A Father's Heart

Love, life, loss, and how
the heart goes on.

by

Edward J. Ferris

Hope Kelley Book Publishing
www.HopeKelleyBookPublishing.com
publish@HopeKelley.com
800.806.6240
Printed in the United States of America

ISBN 9780578751030

ISBN 978-0-578-75103-0

9 780578 751030

A Father's Heart

A Father's Heart

TABLE OF CONTENTS

DEDICATION

"Madeline Nicole, you are my inspiration. They say the brightest lights burn the fastest. This is for you.

EJ, your strength and resolve through all you have endured inspires me to be a better dad and a better man. You are amazing! Thank you for allowing my Father's Heart to continue to love in a way I never thought possible.

To Monica, for your unwavering love, and for motivating me to tell this story. Thank you for providing the opportunity to have a Father's Heart.

To my father, for showing me how to love with more than just my heart, and how to live by faith.

To my brother, John, for modeling selflessness and for all your support and guidance throughout the years.

To my brother, Jim, for giving me the best advice by telling me to never lose my sense of humor."

~~ Edward J. Ferris

FOREWORD

Knowing his struggle to find the right person to write
the Foreword for his book, I responded quickly
and enthusiastically. You see, Edward Joseph Ferris is
my youngest child, my pride and joy.
Ed and I share a bond different from his brothers and
sisters. Not better, just a different quality.

We had a shared appreciation of "my era" of music.
He was only 8 years old when from the back seat of
our '73 Ford Mustang he nonchalantly identified
"String of Pearls" by the Benny Goodman Orchestra
coming from the car's cassette player when I could not
recall the title.

We were both college athletes. As a University of Iowa
Hawkeye, I played both baseball and basketball. As a
Texas Christian University Horned Frog, he performed
on multiple fields, as well. Not as a baseball or football
or basketball player. No, he was a cheerleader. For
someone who grew up in the 1920's and 30's, having
your son tell you he was going to be a cheerleader was
a shock. When I witnessed his practices and
performances, that shock turned to a quiet pride.
Cheerleaders are true athletes. It is doubtful any of the
glamor sports athletes could backflip the length of
Amon Carter Field and, after running back to the
starting position, hoist a co-ed high over his head,
arms extended to allow her to complete the movements
of a cheer designed to bring the crowd to its feet.

As the youngest, Ed was afforded special privileges.
Discipline was neither as swift nor severe as his
older brothers experienced. This was not because his
mother and I were worn down after a 16-year

span of having children and just too tired to respond. No, the reason was much more precise.

Between the birth of his next older brother and Ed, his mother and I lost five children. His birth was a miracle. To his mother and I, it was also a message from God that we were not abandoned. Joy had returned to our family. Sadly, we also share the searing unimaginable pain of losing a child. Much like he did with his choice of athletic endeavors, he has chosen a different path for his grief.

Whereas I kept it all in, not allowing anyone to witness my grief, standing firm and being outwardly strong, Ed reveals his grief in the following pages. It is a difference between us I applaud. Just as I did when he completed his gymnastics and feats of strength on the sidelines of the football fields and basketball courts.

The reason is this. By sharing his grief, his joys, his triumphs, and his tragedies through his words rather than remaining proudly stoic, he will touch the lives of parents who share the frustration of struggling to heal their child, or the heart breaking grief of losing a child. A loss no parent should ever endure. He will let them know they are not alone. He will, perhaps, guide them through their own dark tunnel.

He knows the grief, the sorrow, and the sadness never go away. However, he also knows the Heavenly Love of a child called home too soon allows the heart to go on. Madi and I, along with the brothers and sisters Ed never met are doing well and await our reunion; all in God's time. I am honored to have been called to write the Foreword to my son's book.

~~Jack Ferris 1920-2000

PROLOGUE

Growing up in semi-rural Midwest in the late 60's and throughout the 70's, feelings and emotions were not something we talked about and certainly did not share. I grew up with an amazing father whose love knew no bounds. He showed his love in many ways. I always knew love was there. I also knew it was not something that was up for discussion.

Dad had a saying I internalized through the years. He was one of the few dentists in a town of 12,000 people but never joined the country club. When we would go to the public golf course or out to eat, invariably someone would say, "Doc, why aren't you at the country club?" In traditional Midwest, self-deprecating fashion, Dad would reply, "Must not be much of a club if they would let me in."

As you might imagine, writing about myself is not something that comes naturally or easily. I am someone my daughter would absolutely NOT classify as an "advertiser". Someone so self-absorbed they are their own favorite topic. However, this story is not about me. Rather, it is about a special part of me I have only shared with those closest to me. I now share it with you.

This is about my heart. It is about the way my heart was formed into a "Father's Heart".   It is about how my heart processed feelings and events over the course of the life and, sadly, death of a child. This is a true story from a singular perspective.   I imagine many will find parts of it eerily familiar. If you do, claim it as your story, your heart.

As Fathers we owe it to each other to be true to our children and admit the love, the fear, the angst, and the pride our heart feels for them.
I would go so far as to say denying or hiding those emotions is to deny your own fatherhood and degrade your humanity.

Regardless, this is the story of my heart, with all the flaws and frailties that come with it.

I hope you enjoy the ride.
~~ Edward J. Ferris

CHAPTER ONE

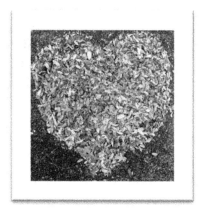

Love
It began early and lasted a lifetime.

From the moment I found out my wife was pregnant, I felt different. Initially, a queasiness in my stomach made me wonder if I was "ready". Can you ever be? How do you define "ready?" Financially stable with a trust fund already set for your young off-spring? Mentally prepared for all the twists and turns of raising a small human and their complete selfishness? Emotionally prepared to see a life spring from your wife's body and be asked to detach said life from said body with a pair of scissors? Come on man, you know you are NEVER "ready".

Or are you? Regardless of your financial, mental, or emotional state of readiness, none of these are the true definition of "ready". Being "ready" is simple and simultaneously complex. The simple part is because it is a straightforward proposition. Complex because, as a guy, it requires us to do something we have been trained to avoid from the time we were wee lads.

To be "ready" to welcome a new life into yours, you need to be prepared to give 100% of yourself to someone else with no thought of "what am I going to get out of this?", with no hesitation to give up anything and everything for that life. If you are prepared to give over your life to theirs, then you are truly "ready."

I can say without hesitation, I was "ready." Those around me thought I had lost what little of a mind I had. Every waking and unconscious thought was about my baby and the woman carrying our child. It is not something easy to explain. You either get it or not. I hope you do.

Once that initial queasy feeling went away and I had the conscious thought I was going to be a father, there was a strange sense of calm and comfort. A feeling I was made for this. A feeling I was going to be amazing at it. I did not then nor do I now claim to be the perfect dad. Far from it. The point is my heart was ready to be given over 100% without any reservation to someone I had not met and had no way of knowing if I would even like once I did.

So many emotions flood the conversation when a baby is about to come into the picture, it becomes hard to distinguish real from fantasy.

Euphoria sweeps over you briefly because something amazingly spectacular is about to happen. Sheer terror takes over because you helped make it happen. You are responsible for the result *for better or worse.* Were they serious all those years ago in the church?   There is intense worry. How are you going to screw this up? How is this going to screw you up?   Those emotions are all real and, brother, did I have plenty of them. But deep down, at the foundation of my soul, I knew. Regardless of the euphoria, the terror, and the worry. My heart would always belong to the tiny little human inside my wife's womb. My heart would never again belong to me.

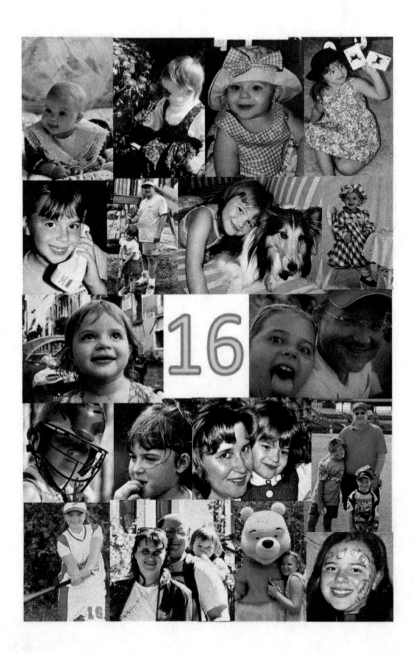

CHAPTER TWO

Every Valentine's Day, I would get a special book for each of my children. On the 21st Anniversary of this tradition, it was time to change things up. The following story was written as my Valentine's gift to my not so little girl.

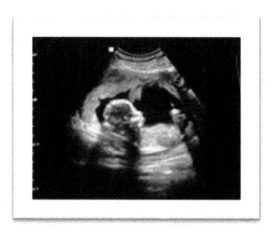

Madi and Me - "The Beginning"

For my special little girl. I love you always and forever. You carry my heart, my hopes, and my prayers with you every day.

It was Love with a capital L from the very first moment.

These days there are questions about the "very first moment." Is it at conception, at birth or somewhere in between? All I can tell you is my first moment was your very first sonogram.

Standing in the doctor's office with your mom on the exam table, her hand in mine our hearts racing with excited anticipation and sheer terror. We looked first at each other, then to the doctor, and finally fixed our gaze on the monitor beside the exam table. It began to whirr, the noise mimicking the way my head was feeling. At first it was just like watching an old TV station that had shut down for the night. Blurry lines going everywhere, and strange noises coming through the speakers. The screen appeared, kind of a dull purple, black and grey. Then the image appeared looking like a solid balloon floating in the haze. "There is the uterus," the doctor said. "And there, there is your b.... a.....b.....y." That word was in slow motion as it made its way through my brain.

Even today those words and the emotion of that moment bring tears to my eyes. Years later, you and EJ still tell me, "You always cry at the TV!" Maybe here is where it started. The picture of my baby on the screen forever changed my life in the best way possible. It is an emotion difficult to explain. There is a warmth inside knowing you created a little life out of love. The hope you will raise your baby into a toddler, a young child, and a teenager. The fear they will one day be an adult. Your job done. You will be cast aside as she builds her own life.

As those thoughts raced through my head, competing for attention in a very few seconds, I noticed a unique sound. One I had never heard before. Rhythmic, almost hypnotic.

The sound of water and the beating of a slightly muffled drum. It was coming from the machine as the doctor took measurements. All at once, we looked at each other and realized, not only is that our baby, but we are listening to our baby's heartbeat!!!

She is real, not just a dream. We created a baby out of love and *that* was my very first moment.

From that day on, my love changed; it deepened, it lengthened, it strengthened. You will never know the true depths of love until you share such a moment with the one you love and with whom you created this new life. Love, and your life, will never be the same. For that I thank God every day. He allowed me to take part in one of the greatest miracles ever. The miracle of life, your life. In the process, He has taught me and challenged me more than I thought possible. He showed me the true meaning and depth of love.

From that very first moment, it was LOVE.

It is not all fun and games.

It is said youth is wasted on the young. Not being so young anymore, I kind of get it. However, there are cases where youth and inexperience work to your benefit. Such was the case when the doctor sat us down three months into the pregnancy and showed us another picture of the life we created. This time, the mood was nowhere near as joyous and the picture was quite clear.

"See this small dot here?" the doctor asked. "That's your baby." OK, so what? We have seen it before. What we had not seen before was the large dark spot on the picture approximately 20X larger than our baby. That large spot, we learned, was placenta previa. Placenta previa happens when the placenta pulls away from the uterus, leaving a gaping hole. We were told any movement could cause the baby to break loose and float into the abyss, causing a miscarriage.

We quickly made a decision. We would do everything possible to protect our baby. Mom would immediately stop working and go to bed... for the next 6 months. We never gave it a second thought. No debate about possible options or life choices.

Our choice was to protect the life of our unborn child without regard to our personal wants or needs. As a parent, when your child is in danger, (particularly when they have no chance to defend themselves), you do whatever is necessary to protect them.

Each day was remarkably similar. Mom would wake up and situate herself in bed. I would arrange pillows in such a way to reduce the stress on her abdomen, while providing comfort for her back and body. You, your mom and EJ still benefit from my considerable skill in pillow stacking.

There was a cooler next to the bed stocked with small drinks and snacks. The remote was always close at hand.

Magazines (pre-internet) and books rounded out the perimeter. Off to work I would go, praying all during the 30-mile drive that my wife and baby were safe at home. I would return around lunch time as often as possible to refresh the cooler, update the reading material and re-align the pillows.

Nighttime was spent either in bed next to Mom or on the couch together after helping her out to the living room. *Friends* was one of the top shows of 1995, but we chose not to partake.

Instead, we would watch *Northern Exposure, Beverly Hills 90210,* (embarrassing to admit), *ER,* Seinfeld, *Frazier,* and *The Nanny.* It would be another 21 years before Mom decided to binge watch (that was not a thing in 1995) *Friends* and think it was one of the best things ever to appear on TV. So much for being hip or current.

Our only other eventful activity was going to doctor's appointments. Driving meant twisting, turning, pushing, and pulling. You guessed it; I was not going to let mom take that risk.

I went to every appointment during those 6-months. The nurses joked that I was there so much they wondered if the appointments were for me or her. I am sure they were as happy as I was when the time arrived.

"It's time..."

Late in the evening of November 2, I heard those words. While they were so very much expected, I was still surprised. Getting the bag in the car and tucking momma and baby into their comfy heated leather seat, my heart was jumping out of my chest. We had a 20+ mile drive to contemplate our collective plus one future and the events that were about to unfold. Similar events happen every day, multiple times per day all around the world. But when you and your loved ones engaged in them, they are intense, they are special, and they are magical.

The drive was one big blur. Mariah Carey was belting out *Vision of Love* from the strategically prepared CD with more than a little help from me. Not sure mom appreciated the accompaniment, but when you are flying down the freeway at 90 plus miles an hour in labor pain, the insufferable singing of the driver is not exactly high on your priority list. She was more concerned about me videotaping the entire trip with our camcorder in one hand, and the other alternating between the steering wheel and her belly. Weaving in and out as is my habit, we arrived at the doors of the Arlington hospital in what had to be record time.

Rumor has it we may have arrived sliding to a stop.

We entered the hospital quite delirious. As they whisked mom off to Labor & Delivery, I was left to do paperwork. After what seemed an eternity, I joined mom in her room for the main event. Hooked up to machines and things beeping all around, everything seemed a bit more mechanical than inspirational. After much breathing, cramping and sweating, we were told something first-time parents hear often. "The pains you are experiencing are phantom labor pains, they are not real, go home and come back when it's time."

There is that phrase again. How are we supposed to know when it is time? How are we supposed to know?! Seemed like it was time several hours ago when we started this glorious journey.

Tails between our legs, we slowly made our way back to the car and then casually back home. Mariah was quiet, the speed was more trot than sprint, the weaving was left to the Thursday night post bar crowd. The mood was decidedly less celebratory and far more subdued.

The adrenaline returned full force in a few short hours. Mariah was cued up. The bag was in the car and off we went for a second time. With fewer cars on the road at this early morning hour, weaving was not necessary. The previous record time was now a distant second. Thankfully, my singing skills were resplendent, especially as compared to the moaning and complaining from the passenger seat.

Serenading and caressing simultaneously at extreme speeds on an empty highway were much easier this time and helped mom stay calm.

Arriving a second time, we found limited staff. I located a wheelchair for the mother to be and still not seeing a candy striper in sight took matters into my own hands. Knowing the drill from just a few hours ago, I headed to Labor & Delivery without delay and with no medical personnel in tow.

CHAPTER THREE

I Did Not Study For This Test

Arriving in Labor and Delivery after having just been there a few hours earlier, we recognized a few friendly faces. We were provided accommodations and mom was hooked up to all the machines once again. Seemed that our previous visit had jaded the staff. They were attentive but appeared as though they expected to be sending us on our way again. While it did take considerably longer than mom and dad would have liked, after a tremendous amount of work, sweat and tears from Mom, our precious baby girl arrived mid-morning. Ten fingers. Ten Toes. Absolutely perfect!!

There are so many stories that could be told of that amazing morning and our time in the delivery suite, but three really stand out.

One was just after we found out our baby was a little girl.   As the announcement was made by the doctor, you were held out in a manner that would later be dubbed the "Simba Cam", raising you up for all to see.   I found out why when I was handed a pair of surgical scissors and asked to do the honors of cutting the umbilical cord.   What?!? You want me to take a sharp object to a part of this precious gem? Oh well, sure, why not?

Taking the scissors in hand and not wanting to mess up, I did just that. Trying to be gentle and do no harm, I only cut through half the cord on my first attempt. Going back a second time, I finally clipped the cord freeing my baby from her mother.   You were taken away to be put under a warmer, cleaned up and wrapped in a blanket.

The second was when Jackie, the nurse, with her wide smile and engaging countenance handed me my daughter for the very first time.

"Ooooh! That girl already has Daddy under her thumb. Look at that pout! Daddy, she has got

Lexus pout. Daddy is in trouble," Jackie said almost singing.

Those may be the most truthful words I heard that day. Not that I heard many. My head was spinning, and my ears could not keep up.

The last and most crucial time was when were asked about a name. Unlike many of our compatriots and virtually everyone today, we chose to wait to find out the sex of our baby until birth. Novel idea, I know, but we loved it. The excitement of having your baby is only exceeded by the anticipation of finding out if you chose the right color for the nursery. As a result, we had not settled on a name. We had several options for both male and female names but had not yet decided on one. With mom a bit foggy, we had to make a decision. Madeline Rene? Meredith Nicole?

What would it be? Oh, the stress!!! What would it be? Together we discussed and decided we liked Madeline Rene. So, there it was. Except, it was not because...well, remember the umbilical cord? Apparently, mom was not the only one a bit foggy and my caution was not relegated strictly to surgical scissors. My mouth suffered a similar fate. When we were asked for the name of our child, Daddy blurted out "Madeline Nicole" without even realizing it. Thus, Madeline Nicole Ferris became the first child of Edward Joseph and Monica Monique Ferris, the two happiest people on the planet on November 3, 1995.

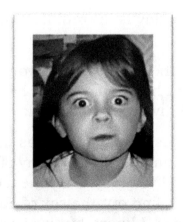

What do you mean we have to go?

Wow, what a whirlwind few months and days. Mom's bedrest, the constant doctor visits, the morning sickness, and restless nights were done.

We now had a beautiful baby girl. We would be able to start enjoying our new family. The exhaustion of the two trips to the hospital, the birth, and numerous visits from friends and family were behind us. Now we could relax. Just as we took a breath, the nurse came in and said, "Ready to go?" WHAT?!? Go where? When? Why? Huh?

No time to enjoy the nice room, the comfort of knowing we were in the loving care of some terrific medical professionals. Our girl was being checked and double checked regularly. Nope, out you go, to the cold hard world of parenthood. No directions, no warranty, no in-home installation, no nothing. Here is your daughter, who at the time looked suspiciously like an albino burrito.

Her hospital issued beanie and blanket wrapping her up tight.

Being escorted away from the security blanket of the hospital, we approached our vehicle with a great deal of trepidation. Did we buy a safe enough car? Volvo, check. Did we put the car seat in right? Rear facing, seemed to be tight, check? Did we install the matrix of mirrors so we can see her from the front seat? Rearview, back window turned slightly to the right, check. Did we get all the various and sundry baby stuff we accumulated from the many visits of friend and family? Check. Trunk packed and shut. Front seat full of all manners of pink, purple and pastel colors of countless outfits, stuffed whatever's and tidbits, check. Ok, off we go. Whoops!!!

Guess I need to get Mom out of the wheelchair and into the car. Sheesh, almost really blew that one.

Remember the laws of physics we broke and land speed records we set on the way? Yeah, there will be none of that on this ride. Interesting how much more careful you are with a baby in a car seat as opposed to the warmth of a mothers' womb. No weaving, full turn signals, proper use of acceleration and deceleration lanes, Mariah still there, but at a volume more appropriate to an elevator. Think back to your very first Drivers' License road test and multiply it by a safety factor of about 10. That is how the ride home went. "Is she okay?", "What's that noise?", "Did she throw up?", "Was that turn ok?", "Why is that car so close?", "Get off my tail you dumba**!" were just some of the words uttered from the driver as we made our way carefully toward Bedford.

As we approached, we realized a proud Grandpa had decorated the exterior of our home to herald the return of his new princess. Banners, balloons, and streamers festooned our garage door. Pulling up to the house, I realized we needed to immortalize this moment on film. Around the block we went and made our second approach. Camcorder at the ready, we announced the triumphant arrival of the castle's newest ruler on film.

A few days later when a friend asked to see the hilarious EJ Frog's Wild Ride video he watched in the hospital room we realized we had taped the climactic arrival over the exciting races to the hospital. One of many dumb little mistakes we would make through the years, but we were home. We were a family. We were about to introduce Madeline to her biggest fans.

CHAPTER FOUR

The Meeting

One of the aspects of Mom's bedrest I failed to mention was her constant companions. Blondie was our loyal and well-travelled cocker spaniel. Samm was our gorgeous sheltie. They were omnipresent and on watch anytime you and Mom were home alone. Blondie had accompanied us when we lived in Germany and on our many weekend trips around Europe. She was confident, cocky and completely in control. Samm was our prim and proper guy. Attentive and alert but toeing the line set by Blondie. Always sleeping along Mom's back to provide heat, support and love, Blondie was amazingly aware of what was happening. She helped comfort mother and child through the entire process. Now it was time to meet face to face.

The door opened and our two pooches were sitting there in great anticipation to see what it was that had kept us away for the last 48 hours. What the heck was in that huge thing Dad was holding?

Walking into the step-down living room, I set the carrier on the floor and the stage was set.

From either side, Blondie and Samm looked at the little burrito, then back at us, then back at the burrito. I was concerned we may just find the package on the floor, unwrapped, dogs licking like there was no tomorrow. Much like we did on Christmas Eve in Ansbach when Blondie found the Christmas lamb basting in the basement while Charlie, Renate, Heidi and Johannes were at Christmas services.

My fears were relieved when both dogs crept ever so slowly up to you, sniffed your face, then your blanket, then your toes and erupted into one of the greatest displays of tail wagging known to man. They realized their baby had arrived and they too were in love!!

Blondie assumed her position as big sister and ultimate protector. When you were sleeping, Blondie would lay directly beneath your crib in such a way to keep an eye on the door to the room as well as the window that looked out to the front door of the house. Samm was only allowed in for special occasions or when Mom or I were there. Otherwise, it was Blondie and Madeline. No one had better dare to come to do harm to her kid. Occasionally, visitors would come when you were sleeping.

Grandma and Grandpa's ability to detect when a grandchild is sleeping restfully, and the parents finally had a moments' peace was legendary. When this would happen, Blondie would first growl lowly as they came up the walk. As they progressed to the step leading to the door and right next to the window she used as her lookout spot, she would, while still under the crib, launch into full blown attack mode. Barking and growling until one of us identified the intruder and gave the all clear.

During all this one thing remained constant. You did not move. When you were asleep, Blondie could do anything in and around the room and you would not flinch. Heaven forbid Mom or I happened to walk by the door on our tip toes. BOOM, you were awake, hungry, fussy, dirty, something requiring attention.

All this work and little sleep was hard on Mom. This new schedule was wearing on her.

You Took Me Where?

And on the Seventh Day, she saw what she created and was pleased, so she rested. Notice, *She* rested, not me. No time to rest for Super DAD, it is November 10.

Today is the first home preseason game for Billy
Tubbs and the 1995-96 TCU Horned Frog
Basketball Team. Your first exposure to Super
FROG!! OK, so at 7 days old, you had no clue, but
still we started you out right.

Grandma, Uncle John, and Aunt Lynne all looked
at me as if to say, "you are going to do what?"
Grandpa, on the other hand, "knew the score" as
he used to like to say. He knew basketball was
life. I excitedly put Grandpa and Grandma in the
car with us and off we went.

In your finest purple accoutrement, you entered
the hallowed halls that once held the likes of
"Goo" Kennedy, Darrel Browder, Dennis Nutt,
Jamie Dixon, Carven Holcombe and Tracy
Mitchell. Daniel Meyer Coliseum was now home
to one Kurt Thomas who had just accomplished a
feat only two other people in history had done
before him. He was the leading scorer and
rebounder in the country for the 1994-95 season.
How could any self-respecting 7-day old pass that
up?

What an amazing feeling to share this great game
with my mother, father, and child. Wow, was
that cool. What was not cool? Still reeling from
the events of the previous week and the
excitement of showing you off, I neglected to think
of how the old ladies with season tickets near ours
would react to such a young child being brought
by her father of all people to a college sporting
event.

"Does this child not have a mother?" "Does he have any idea how to change a diaper?" "That poor baby should be at home, it has to be past her bedtime."

These had to be some of the thoughts wafting through the rafters at Daniel Meyer as the bitties glared their disapproving eyes in my direction. Confident in my skills, I walked down the aisle, baby in hand – both hands, and took our seat for what would be the last season of basketball in the Southwest Conference.

Grandpa was so proud that night. His Granddaughter was watching. Well, okay... in attendance, at his favorite sporting event with his favorite team wearing his favorite color and for the topper, irritating the old ladies. What a night!!!

To add a bit of kismet, I noticed that we were sitting in seat 7 on the 7th day of your life. Care to guess what came next? Exactly, I pried the number plate off the seat and presented it to you. I am proud to say it sits in your jewelry box to this very day.

That was the first of many adventures to come in a lifetime of amazing stories, some still to be told, others still to be lived and loved.

CHAPTER FIVE

Life
Growing up Madeline

Her first basketball game was one of the many adventures Madeline would have as she grew from a baby, into a toddler, and eventually a teenager.

Even from a young age, Madeline was... shall we say, a little bossy.   Her mother called her, "My Little CEO." She never shied away from anything and took control of everything.

One example was the relationship between she and one of her earliest and best friends, Lauren. How two kids so dramatically different could become such a tight pair was amazing. You see, as a young girl, Lauren would talk to NO ONE!! She barely talked to her parents. She would absolutely not talk to any other adult under any circumstances and only sparingly to other kids in the neighborhood.

Madeline, on the other hand, would talk a blue streak to anyone that would listen and some that would not. No matter the subject, she had an opinion on everything and was not shy about sharing.

Somehow, Madeline and Lauren became the best of friends. As they entered Kindergarten, Madeline and Lauren were inseparable, which was a good thing.

Lauren would not talk to any of her teachers nor most of the kids in the class.

If she needed anything Madeline was her mouthpiece. Somehow Madeline knew what Lauren wanted or needed and made sure she got it through any means necessary.

When they got home, Madeline became the informer. Not in a bad way, rather in a helpful way. Lauren's mother wanted to know what interesting things were happening at school. Lauren sat tight lipped. Madeline would rattle on endlessly about their day, answering questions with gusto and in great detail. Madeline was always up on the latest because the teachers trusted her to shuttle information between the classrooms and main office. It was the same story all through their elementary school years. Madeline never minded or really thought too much about it. Lauren was her friend and she was doing what friends do.

As loyal as Madeline was to her friends, she was equally fierce to those she felt had done wrong or not worthy of her trust.

One day, Madeline and her friends were playing in the neighborhood park. She had taken her little brother, EJ, along. EJ was five years younger but relished playing with the older girls and keeping up with them. Madeline never shut him out or let anyone keep him from being a part of the group. As they climbed and slid and jumped and ran, EJ ended up on a platform that was about three and a half feet off the ground. That may not have seemed like much to the 6-7-year-old girls, but to an 18-month old kid it looked like he was at the edge of the Grand Canyon.

Before EJ could call to Madeline for help, one of the kids Madeline felt unworthy of her trust proved Madeline correct. She ran up from behind EJ, placed two hands firmly in his back, extended her arms and shoved him off the platform.

Down he went. Landing with a thud, followed by wails and screams of pain, EJ curled up in a ball grabbing what we would find out later was his broken leg. As his mom rushed to his side to comfort him, Madi turned and ran full speed to the top of the platform to defend her brother and to confront the perpetrator. Madeline was not going to let anyone hurt her EJ.

While Madeline was exceptionally protective of her little brother, they were insanely competitive.

Their competitiveness would lead us on a journey that would dominate our lives for the next ten years.

From the time EJ could walk, he was always athletic. Being a lefty, I put a baseball in his hand very early and whoa did that kid have an arm. He could really sling it. When he was three, we were playing in the front yard. He with his little plastic bat, me putting whiffle balls on a tee at first and then pitching to him. To this day, I marvel at his hand/eye coordination and how he sees things from an athletic perspective. His mom came out and I said, "hey, take a look at this."

As I pitched to EJ he would hit the ball solidly and smile that devilish smile of his. Mom was impressed and gushed about her son. Suddenly, Madeline, who we did not know was watching and listening, came from behind her mother and said, "Give me that!" She took the bat from EJ's hands and told him to get out of the way. EJ was irritated, Monica was furious, and I was curious. At eight years old, Madeline swam on the neighborhood swim team, played tennis and rode horses, but had not shown much of an interest in traditional team sports. Today, she was not going to let her brother get all the attention and accolades.

As she grabbed the bat and took her position, I said, "Want to start with the tee?"

"Nope" was the curt response.

As I prepared to loft the first pitch, Madi assumed a stance I can only describe as picture perfect. With a determined look on her face, she swung at aggressively at the first pitch and sent it whistling past my right ear. Hmmm, I thought. Beginner's luck? Second pitch was lined into the bushes down what would have been first base. Third pitch over my head onto the neighbor's driveway some eighty feet away. Remember folks, these are whiffle balls being hit by an eight-year-old girl that had never picked up a bat.

Mom says, "Hey maybe you should try softball" and the rest is history......well kind of.

Becoming Madi

Madeline signed up for little league and was put on a team with girls she had never met before. I agreed to help coach as I had played baseball in high school and made a feeble attempt at college ball. To say Madeline stood out in the early practices would be an understatement. She did. She was HORRIBLE!! I told Monica this experiment would not last long. For the first game, the coach put her in right field.

Anybody that has ever played baseball or softball knows what that means. Early in the game a ground ball rolled between the 1st and 2nd basemen toward right. Nothing fast, just an easy roller that got past two eight-year old girls. As the ball casually rolled toward Madeline, I remember thinking, "that's slow enough, stay in front of it and you will be fine." Madeline sees the ball roll between the infielders surveys the situation turns and runs away. She ran away from a ball rolling slowly toward her on the ground!!! We got home that night and I told Monica, "Tennis it is".

The next morning, I asked Madeline what she thought of her first softball game, expecting to have a dejected little face tell me she hated it.

"Daddy, I want to be a pitcher!" was the reply.

Wait, what did she just say? Pitcher? You mean the one that stands thirty-five feet from someone with a bat, throws an 11" ball and hopes they don't knock it back down your throat?

After gathering my jaw off the floor, I composed myself, thought for a minute and said, "Are you sure?"

"Yep, I want to control the game," the little CEO said.

As any good dad will attest, when your daughter wants something you do not tell her "No." You find a way to make her realize it is not what she really wants or the work it will take to get it will be too hard. That way when she decides against it, it is her decision and you are not seen as the bad guy. A plan must be hatched quickly.

"Ok, Madeline, this is what I think. You looked bad out there yesterday and I am afraid to put you in that position. But, if it is something that you really want, I will do what I can to help make it happen. Before I do that, you have to do a few things first."

I proceeded to lay out five things that Madeline would need to demonstrate a proficiency in before we would even talk about pitching again. Secure in the knowledge there was no way in the world she would follow through and I just pulled the best dad move of all time. I looked into her big brown eyes and said, "You understand the deal?"

"OK!" was the happy retort and off she went. Um, uh.... that was not what I was expecting.

From that day forward, a switch flipped. She wanted something and would not be denied. She went after each task with determination and focus.

Be able to play catch with me from 60' for :15 and not miss a catch or make a bad throw, check. Be able to field 10 sharp ground balls in rapid succession with proper form and make a throw from second base to first without an error, check.

Be able to stand in the batter's box with a pitching machine throwing 40 mph with confidence, check.

Be able to bunt five consecutive 35 mph pitches in fair territory, alternating between the first and third baseline, check. Make at least two positive defensive plays with no errors and get a hit in the same game, check.

The list I thought would end this crazy talk was completed inside of three weeks. Thus, began an odyssey of blood, sweat, tears, amazing memories of triumph, tribulation, and great friendships. At that moment, she became Madi.

Softball tested Madi. She was not a big or strong kid, so she had to understand fundamentals and leverage to achieve the necessary power on the mound or at the plate.

She was not fast of foot, so she had to study the game and her opponents to read body language and anticipate what was going to happen to be in the right place at the right time and make the play. She did not stand out visually as an athlete, so she had to be fearless and tenacious to be noticed.

Softball also brought out the best in Madi. She was a straight A student, so she used her brain to out-think her opponent. She was an extreme extrovert, so she used that to rally her team and disarm the opponent with kindness off the field.

She was intensely competitive, so from the first pitch, she left it all on the field. She wanted to earn everything she got. So much so that if we received a "participant ribbon" or any trophy that was not first place. or she did not think we deserved, it ended up in the trash can at the exit to the park. She was definitely not *an Everybody gets a Trophy* kind of kid.

Make way for Bubbles.

As hard as Madi could be, she exuded an amazing joy and love of life that caused people to be drawn to her. We played local tournaments two or three times per month. One weekend as the girls were finishing warm-ups, I went inside to do my preparation for the game.

Entering the building, a woman noticed my shirt and excitedly said, "The SLAM!! Are you playing now?"

"Yes Ma'am." I answered. "Field 3."

"Is that girl pitching?" she asked

"Well, yes Ma'am, they are all girls" I said, laughing to myself.

"No, the little one. The one that blows bubbles when she pitches, she is so much fun to watch."

"Yes Ma'am, she is. That is my daughter. We call her Bubbles."

"I just love watching her." she says as she moves to the counter.

"Thank you, good luck today." I said as we parted ways.

When I got back to the dugout, I was still laughing. Madi asked me why. I quickly told her the story and she giggled a bit as she blew a bubble.

In the second inning, Bubbles ran into a little trouble. She had runners on first and second with one out. She was frustrated because her pitches were not breaking or locating the way she wanted. She decided to try a little harder, over-cooked one and drilled the girl right in the hip. Madi immediately covered her face to hide a secret that only she and I knew. With her glove obscuring her face, her shoulders started to shake. Everyone is the stands felt bad thinking she was upset. As fans and teammates alike tried to encourage her, from our stands comes this unfamiliar thundering voice, 'COME ON BUBBLES!! YOU GOT THIS!"

I turn to see who it is. It is the lady from the concession stand in the middle of our fans, standing up, hot dog in one hand, and a drink in the other screaming for Bubbles at the top of her lungs. Madi was so shocked she dropped her glove and revealed her secret. She was not upset. She was laughing hysterically.

For some unknown reason, from the very first time Madi hit a batter, she would burst out laughing. The crowd was a bit stunned and amused.

With the ball in her hand, she pointed to the stands as if to say, "Is that her?"

I shook my head as she laughed some more and blew a bubble. The crowd chuckled with her and she proceeded to get us out of the inning with no runs scored. She had a great time but knew how to buckle down and get it done.

She was also champion of the underdog. Being considered too short or too small, she hated when people judged her without knowing her or giving her a chance to prove herself. One weekend she had the chance to meet one of her pitching idols. She also was one of the sports most accomplished and awarded pitchers.

Madi excitedly stood in line for an autograph. When she got to the front of the line that pitcher looked at Madi and said, "What's up shorty?". Madi looked at her, pulled her hand back that held the ball she was going to ask the pitcher to sign and walked away. We were not allowed to mention that pitchers name in our house again.

Madi applied that principled approach to everyone. Today they say if you can be anything, be kind. Madi was ahead of her time.

Walking out of the ballpark one day, Madi and her mom passed a game that caught her eye. Madi did not know the teams nor anyone on them.

The players were probably five or six years younger than her. She stopped anyway as her mom walked onward toward the car.

After ten or so steps, Monica realized Madi was not by her side. She turned around to go back.

"What are you doing?" her mom asked.

"I want to watch this girl."

"Know her?"

"No," Madi said, never taking her eyes off the field.

Mom, a bit confused said, "Okay, guess I'll watch too."

As they watched the girl, it was obvious she was a young, maybe first-time pitcher. She was small, with fire in her eyes and coaches and fans on her back. They thought they were being supportive. They had no idea how their words were being heard and processed by the young pitcher. Madi did and it made her mad.

The game ended with the mystery girls' team losing 10-2. Monica headed toward the car again, but Madi stayed behind. She waited for the coach to talk to his team and dismiss them. She then walked up to the girl and talked to her for about ten minutes. They both made some pitching gestures, laughed, and shared a big hug before Madi made her way to the car.

When Monica asked Madi what that was all about, Madi just said, "Nothing, I just saw something in her and wanted to tell her not to quit. We all have bad days."

Madi did not know that girl but the girl definitely knew Madi. She was grateful Madi would take an interest and invest time in a younger player she did not even know. That was Madi. Mom's Little CEO taking control and doing what needed to be done.

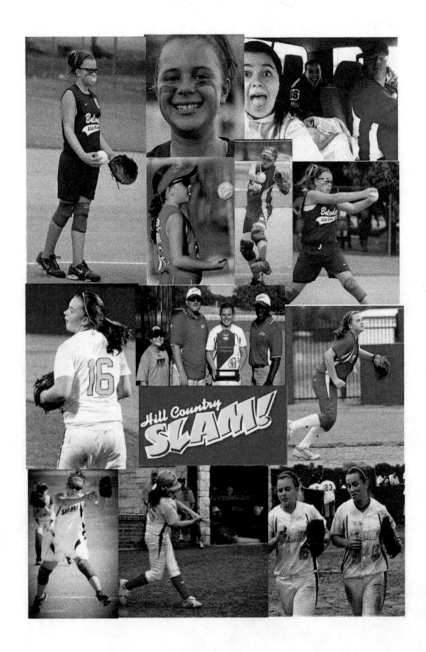

CHAPTER SIX

She Was A Fierce Competitor

When Madi stepped on the field, there was only one thing to be done, WIN. More accurately, DON'T LOSE. Many do not understand the distinction. Our girls did. Before every season, I would tell the girls I only expected one thing, DON'T LOSE!!! The new girls would be in shock and the returnees would laugh.

Our team, The Hill Country SLAM, shout out to Toby Mac who wrote the song we adopted as our team name and motto, was made up of mostly cast-offs, second chance or unknown kids that the name teams did not want. We most definitely *"brought it like it ain't been brung!"*

Our objective was to have every player put everything they have into every practice and into every game. Because the sum of our parts was always stronger than any of our individual players, if everyone went out, gave it everything they had on every play, we were winners.

Regardless of the score we could walk off the field with our heads held high.   The great news is that while we occasionally fell short of our goal, striving for it allowed us to win a lot of games. Even games no one thought we could or should.

One such game happened when she was 13. Madi was pitching against an extremely competitive team in Houston.   Because of the make-up of our team, we, especially Madi, had a HUGE chip on our shoulders. We relished beating "Elite" teams. Theoretically, those teams had all the talent and felt we should not be on the same field with them.   This particular game and this particular team fit that profile perfectly.

Our team was playing great. Madi was pitching out of her mind. We went into the last inning down two runs.   With two out and a runner on second, Madi came to the plate.   Coaching first base, I was trying to find the right words of encouragement and motivation.   Our third base coach was giving her the signals.   She worked the count to 3-1.

An inside pitch came in hot and hard.   She could not quite get out of the way.

"Strike Two!" called the umpire.

He determined the ball hit off the bottom of the bat making it a foul ball and the second strike.

I went nuts! "Come on Madi, get out of the way! That was ball four!"

She looked at me with a very odd look and slowly shook her head ever so slightly from side to side. We were down to one pitch and one out. The payoff pitch was on the way and it looked great. As I followed the ball to Madi, I saw her turn her shoulders to bunt. Even worse, she took her left hand off the bat to attempt a one-handed bunt!! WHAT? She has never bunted one-handed before in her life! If it is a foul, we lose. If she misses it, we lose. If she somehow gets the bunt down and gets thrown out at first base, we lose.

Madi, the slowest player on our team, is now bunting with 2 outs, 2 strikes, down by 2! The bunt surprises everyone and she puts the ball in play.

I am screaming like a mad man at first base, "RUN, COME ON GET HERE!"

With everything seemingly in slow motion, Madi beat out the throw and was safe at first. Everyone was so shocked, our runner from second scored with ease. Down one, and a runner on first, we were still alive.

Ecstatic and a bit befuddled, I turned to congratulate Madi on an amazingly gutsy play. As she stopped running and turned back to first base, I could see HUGE tears running down her face. These were not tears of joy. This kid was hurt, and she was hurt badly.

Turns out strike two did not hit her bat, it hit her hand. Her hand was already twice the size it should be and the most amazing shades of purple.

She could not grip the bat. A one-handed bunt was the only option she could think of. She made a split-second decision and executed a play to keep her team in the game.

Madi was replaced at first with a courtesy runner and returned to the bench for some ice. The courtesy runner scored, tying the game. The game was going into extra innings. What were we going to do? Madi was pitching out of her skull and we had a decision to make.

Through the dugout fence, the head coach asked, "Is it OK? Can you go?"

Her answers were emphatic, quick and to the point.

"No!" and "You aren't taking me out. It's my left hand. I'm finishing this," Madi stated forcefully.

After gently sliding the glove onto Madi's oversized hand, I gave the catcher specific instructions to roll the ball back to her after each pitch so she would not have to endure the pain of the ball smacking the glove. The corners had to cover anything hit her way. Two innings later we won the game. Two hours later the X-rays came back. Her hand was broken.

What did Madi say? "It was worth it!"

Something as insignificant as a broken hand would not stop Madi. She had a focused intensity to achieve and overcome any challenge put in front of her. And she was good at it.

CHAPTER SEVEN

Something Is Not Right

Madi's Freshman year in high school started with a great amount of excitement and anticipation in the air. She was transitioning from travel to high school ball. Her team was expected to be one of the best in the state.

During the short drive to school in the mornings, Madi would mumble to herself as if attempting to memorize an assignment instead of talking to her mom like she always had. She was intense, focused on something important. Once the mumbling started it would not stop until Madi was done. Monica and I talked about it and wrote it off to the stress of starting high school, expecting to contribute on the field and the importance of the upcoming showcase tournament.

One of the biggest recruiting events of the year was coming up in a few short weeks. She wanted to make a good showing for college coaches and start planning her future. She talked about going to Harvard and studying law. She was interested in and knowledgeable about politics and world events. She also wanted to play Division I Softball. Some of the best teams in the country were in our back yard. Those coaches would be at the showcase. Now was the time to make an impression.

Madi had her eye on one specific school and was hoping to have a conversation with their coach.

The school was only a few hours away, had strong academics and had recently made it to the Women's College World Series.

On the Tuesday before the showcase, Madi was practicing with her high school team. They were running a drill where players would high step between the rungs and outside the rails of a real ladder. Madi did not lift her foot quite high enough to clear the ladder, clipped it and her foot hit the ground oddly. Instantly, a sharp pain shot from her foot all the way up her leg. Madi sat out a short time and, despite the pain and weakness in her foot, finished the practice. The next day at travel practice she told me and the Head Coach she was having trouble pushing off her foot during warm-ups. She relayed the story of the ladder, we checked out her foot and took her for an x-ray. Sure enough, her foot was fractured. Her shot at impressing the coaches at the showcase was over.

Despite the setback, Madi made the trip with the team. On the first day, she and I were walking down the sidewalk toward the main venue when we noticed a man walking toward us. We recognized him as the head coach Madi wanted to impress.

As Madi hobbled forward on her crutches and boot, I said, "Hi Coach, how are you today?"

"Fine", he said, "but doesn't look like Madi is doing very well."

Excuse me......did he just say Madi without us even introducing ourselves? What the....?

"No sir, I broke my foot in practice." Madi said, her voice as strong as can be.

"That's too bad, I was really looking forward to watching you this weekend." He said. "Good luck and get healed up."

"Thank you, sir." Madi said, a slight waver now apparent in her voice.

As we parted, Madi hobbled over to a nearby bench, sat down and broke down in tears. She noticed her recruiting profile in his hands. He had read her bio. He knew her. He wanted to see her play and she was on crutches. She was devastated.

She asked if we could have a trainer tape her foot. She would suck it up and find a way to play. She wanted to show him she was the kind of athlete and competitor his university needed. None of those things happened. She sat with her team while they played and other coaches watched. We did not see him for the rest of the weekend.

Madi's return to school that Monday was rough. Not only had she lost the chance to impress her desired college coach, she had to tell her high school coach that she was out for 4-6 weeks. That time was crucial as it was the time of year when coaches made roster and position decisions.

Madi would not have won the starting pitcher spot on varsity regardless. But she had a good bat, played multiple positions, and was a smart base runner. She had a good shot to make it as a reserve. That did not happen either.

When Madi did come back from the injury, she was a not quite herself. We assumed it was a residual effect from her broken foot or the disappointment of not being on varsity. Why would the foot impact her decision making and mechanics? Why would she not use the snub as motivation to earn that spot back?

Movements that were once second nature were now a struggle to her. Her ability to anticipate and react were not up to her standards. Her studies were falling behind as well. The kid that could ace any test without really trying was now studying 4-5 hours at night and getting B's.

Things went on that way for the rest of the year. Something was not right.

Now what?

With Madi fighting to overcome her struggles and finish her freshman year, Monica began having some serious medical concerns.

Monica started experiencing a sharp pain in the back of her head in early January. Her primary doctor provided some relief, but it was only fleeting. More testing and specialists were needed.

In April, Monica was diagnosed with a brain tumor. I still remember taking the call. While driving home after the initial MRI, not more than twenty minutes after the test, my cell phone rang. Looking down and recognizing the number, my heart sank. The news was not going to be good. Monica had a pituitary adenoma.

The neurosurgeon reviewed the MRI and agreed it was likely a pituitary adenoma but could also be something else. Monica's only symptom was the head pain. She did not exhibit any significant visual disturbances, so it was not acting like a typical tumor.

He had operated on patients with a similar medical history and MRI only to find the identified "tumor" was simply inflammation and there was nothing to be removed. We needed to rule that out before he would proceed.

Monica was referred to a neuro-ophthalmologist for further testing. The first appointment was a marathon session. After an initial examination, we were sent back to the waiting room. Monica's name was called a second time and we went in for another evaluation, then another, and then we were told to wait again. A final test was completed, and we were told we needed to go to another office that afternoon for more testing. The tests at that office were different but the process the same. Arriving home after 5:00pm and still in pain, Monica went straight to bed.

The next day was a tournament Saturday for Madi, so we left early. We came back late and left early again on Sunday. We were in the loser's bracket. EJ was left in charge of mom. He sat next to her holding her hand, watching TV, and feeding the dogs. He did a great job. We made it to the Championship game and got home late Sunday night. We walked through the door to a ringing phone.

The neuro-ophthalmologist called personally on a Sunday night. The tumor was confirmed.

Initially, the neurosurgeon wanted to attempt to treat Monica with medication. The medicine seemed to help reduce the pain but never eliminated it. In June, Monica's head pain quickly went from what most of us would consider a headache, to a migraine and crippling pain in about two hours. The tumor had to be removed and quickly.

Surgery was long, but successful. The tumor had wrapped itself around the optic nerve and had to be carefully pulled away. One wrong move and Monica's vision could be severely damage. She could have been rendered permanently blind.

Thanks to the incredible skill of a gifted surgeon, she would still see her children grow up. I often wonder if there are times she wishes she had not seen what was about to happen.

The Transition

Having spent the better part of 2012 focused on Monica and her brain tumor, we entered the summer with a sense of relief and renewal.

While Monica's rehab was still ongoing, Madi and EJ would benefit from a Mother's love and I would be able to grow old with my best friend and the love of my life.

Could it have been relief and renewal led us down the wrong path?

Could our diverted attention have caused us to not see what was happening right in front of our eyes?

Life continued forward. EJ playing hockey. Madi playing softball. Monica resting and recuperating from brain surgery and me trying to keep things "normal"

My plate was full. Madi had her typical summer schedule. Softball practice three times per week, pitching lessons once, hitting lessons once and tournaments most weekends. EJ was focused on hockey tryouts for the travel team. He was going to camps, open skates, and stick and puck as often as he could. Thankfully, Madi had her driver's license.

Madi driving changed our dynamics. I still coached the SLAM, but was not at all her workouts, or her hitting and pitching lessons. Instead, I relied on her to tell me how things went and what she was working on. Madi, being the only one that knew what she was dealing with and realizing what I had just been through with her mom, was not exactly forthcoming with all the details.

The reality was that her pitching and hitting were not improving. In fact, her skill set was degrading across the board. Her other coaches, while somewhat concerned, had seen similar situations before and assumed it was burnout. Madi had been playing softball for eight years straight, 30-35 weekends a year, 5-9 games per weekend.

She was also driving or flying from San Antonio to Houston or Dallas or Oklahoma or Colorado or Florida.

Many times, when kids have been so focused on a single sport for so long and then get the freedom of a drivers' license, they lose interest in that sport and move on to other things. If they stay involved in sports, their parents are the driving force. The scholarship potential, notoriety and popularity, living their lives vicariously through their children. It is something coaches see all the time. The attrition in competitive youth sports between ages 15-17 is astronomical.

That was not Madi. She wanted this more than anything. She had plans. She had goals. She had dreams. Every single one included excelling in softball. Every single one included excelling in the classroom. Every single one of them included getting into a good college, playing softball, and winning championships. Most had her starting or running a company. Others had her becoming a Senator or even President. This kid did not dream small. Every fiber of her being was committed to those plans, goals, and dreams. She was not burned out. She had not lost the fire in her belly. She was fighting for her life.

The Fight Had Already Begun

Prior to her Freshman year, Madi noticed some significant changes with her brain. She could not process thoughts and actions the way she always had. Her body would not always respond the way she wanted it to. She began to have cognitive and balance issues. Rather than share those challenges with us, she was determined to fight through them, to figure out what was happening and to overcome them on her own.

The muttering on the car rides was her way of telling herself what needed to be done that day and prepare for her first period class. She was mentally walking herself into the school, down the hall, counting the doors to make sure she went into the right class. She was playing out the scenario for every class that day. She was reminding herself of the names of her teachers and what assignments she was supposed to turn in to which teachers.

The broken foot was not a result of a misstep with a ladder, but simply a deteriorating body giving way and a bone breaking under otherwise normal circumstances.

She had been dealing with something we could not possibly comprehend. Madi had been battling an unknown foe for several years. Madi confided this to her mother in late 2015. Much too late.

Madi hated not knowing why these things were happening. The only thing worse would have been to admit to someone else she did not know what was happening, much less why. Thus, the clandestine cover-up continued. Madi would provide perfectly logical explanations about these strange happenings or simply present them as a joke or a clumsy step. With her former quick wit and silly nature, she was always doing goofy things. When these things became unintentional, it was not obvious. What should have been obvious was that Madi was in trouble.

On the softball field, she would miss signs and forget counts. You could see her laboring. She struggled to do the things that were once easy for her. She was still competing and performing, just not to her level.

After weekend games, Mondays became like clockwork. She would wake up congested and unable to breathe. Her body ached as if she was 50-years old and she was completely exhausted.

During the summer, she could rest until her next practice or lesson. When school started, it was a different story. It got so bad the attendance people at her high school wondered if we were making up excuses. They called me to ask if she had some special Monday event that kept her from attending school. No, there was not a secret event. Her body was rebelling against her, and no one knew why.

Her doctor said it was allergies and depression.

"Nothing that you don't see in most teenagers these days," he would say.

To which we would say, "But she is not a typical teen. She loves life, she likes school, she is motivated by sports. She has lofty goals."

The doctor looked at us as if we were oblivious parents portraying our daughter as we wished her to be rather than how she really was.

We had no way of knowing how many times that conversation and those looks would play out over the next few years.

The Fight Intensifies

As we watched Madi struggle, she changed before our eyes. The vibrance she brought to life, the energy she added to any situation, the smile that would light up any room started to fade. Our Bubbles was being taken away from us.

She decided to stop playing high school softball. Some saw this as weak and confirmation she did not have what it took to succeed or did not want it badly enough. Nothing could be further from the truth. She wanted it so badly she could not stand by and watch it disappear from her sight because of her own performance. Especially when that performance was being impacted by something outside her control. It was the strongest signal that something was seriously wrong, but we missed it.

She told us she wanted to focus on education. We moved her to a college prep school that would challenge her academically, provide the foundation for her future and the best chance at academic excellence.

With only school to focus on, she started to get back some of the sharpness that once defined her. We started to see the old Madi emerge if only in small ways. She was a breath of fresh air and a welcome addition to the new school. She made friends easily. They were impacting her life and she theirs in positive ways. She decided she wanted to play softball at the new school. Bubbles was making a comeback. She had strung five good months together. There would not be a sixth.

January of 2013, the flu was raging in Texas, especially at her school. We had taken a late Christmas vacation, so Madi did not get back to school until later in the month. By that time, over fifty percent of the students either were sick or had been. We had no idea what had happened while we were gone. We certainly did not know the impact it would have on the rest of her life.

After the first day, Madi let us know what was happening at school. We told her to be careful. Do not drink from the water fountains and wash her hands constantly. If anyone near her was sick, move away. The typical stuff. When she came home at the end of the week, she said she did not feel well and went right to bed. We did not know it then, but that was the last time she would attend a full day of school. EVER!

Madi was tested for the flu. It was negative. She was given Tamiflu as a preventative and with the hopes it may help her feel a bit better. The doctor said she should start to feel better in a couple of days. Not only did she not feel better, she felt worse.

This time off to the Emergency Hospital and more testing. Nope, no flu, no strep.

This time they just said to her, "You are just dehydrated and may have a virus that we cannot pinpoint, you should feel better in 5-7 days."

Three days later, Madi began to feel worse, started having her first ever nose bleeds and a headache like she had never known before.

On the second day of nose bleeds and headaches, we called the Emergency Hospital and asked if she should come back.

"She needs a CT. We do not have that equipment here. She needs to go to the hospital." was the reply.

Off to the hospital we went expecting to get to the bottom of this. Arriving at the hospital, Madi was triaged and checked into a room. They did the obligatory questioning which included the alcohol and drug use, sexual activity, and suicidal tendencies.

Madi actually thought it was funny they asked her if it was OK if we stayed in the room for the questions.

She looked at them and said, "Why wouldn't it be?"

Standard ER protocols were followed, blood pressure, heart rate and blood test were completed. The doctor looked in her eyes, ears, evaluated her condition and gave her the migraine protocol. Her diagnosis was a simple migraine with nose bleeds. The migraine protocol made her sleepy but had no impact on her pain. In the face of direct evidence showing a CT to be appropriate and us begging for one, no CT was performed.

"It's a nosebleed, kids get them, if I ordered a CT every time someone had a headache or nosebleed I would have to answer to the hospital." was the direct quote from the doctor.

The doctor was right about one thing. Madi got nose bleeds from time to time. However, the one thing she was wrong about was the pain. For the remainder of her life Madi would live with head pain.

Three days later we took her to a Level 1 Trauma Center. The head pain had worsened to the point Madi was curled up in a ball crying unable to stand without assistance. Madi was placed in an isolation room. They thought she may have meningitis. The doctors wanted to take every precaution. She was given heavy dose medications, received a CT and underwent what she would eventually say was the most painful thing she ever experienced. Madi received two spinal taps performed bedside in the ISO room with her mom and I watching. Because they did not get enough fluid on the first one, a second needle had to be jammed into her spine while she lay helpless, crying, and holding my hand. Poor kid.

They gave her a Toradol shot, hoping it would relieve some of the pain. It did not. In fact, over the next few weeks, the injection site, (her right thigh), would start losing feeling. It never returned.

Once the tests were completed and the results evaluated by the doctors, they came into the room and said, "The tests do not show any abnormality. We cannot be sure but think what you have is viral. You won't likely die from it, so we are going to discharge you."

Driving away from a hospital, once again, after arriving with high hopes for some sort of resolution or plan of action, the mood was very somber and heavy. Madi lay in the back seat, in the fetal position, eyes closed, sunglasses on, covered with a blanket. Monica in the passenger seat trying to hide the tears rolling down her cheeks. Me, driving in a mental fog. How am I going to fix this? Where can I turn to get answers and take this pain away from my little girl? It was not the first such drive and it would not be the last.

The Battle Raged On

There is no way to adequately describe Madi's life over the next four years. We lived it and still find it unbelievable. Our family watched us go from doctor to doctor, from specialist to specialist, and from hospital to hospital desperately searching for answers. They could not begin to fathom it.

It is inconceivable what Madi must have felt. The constant pain in her head. The various maladies she suffered hitting her on all fronts. Her young life stolen. Maybe this countdown will help you understand just a bit better. Be thoughtful and take your time.

Now....
Picture your 5 favorite things.
Picture your 4 favorite people.
Picture your 3 favorite places.
Picture your 2 favorite outfits.
Picture your heart's 1 deepest desire.
Picture the memories, burned them into your mind. Now close your eyes for 30 seconds.

When you open your eyes, your life contains none of those things. Your favorite things and people have been removed from your life. The places you loved to go in the clothes that make you feel special are beyond your reach or too uncomfortable. The dreams you have been striving to achieve your entire life, that were once within your grasp, have been ripped from your reality. Worse yet, they remain vivid in your memory. Mental and physical reminders all around you of what was and of what could have been... what should have been... what cannot be.

That had to be the way it was for Madi. One moment she was on top of the world. In what seemed like the blink of an eye, it was all gone. Madi was a voracious reader. She would read almost anything, but loved biographies of successful people, mysteries that required the reader to envision the scene and attempt to solve the crimes along the way and, of course, all the typical teenage reading that she would discuss with her friends. She would go to the library constantly and get 4-5 books at a time. Three days later she was back there doing the same thing. Once the headaches began, she was limited to a few paragraphs a week. It was just too painful.

Madi loved to watch movies, especially those that made her think. When we would watch as a family, she and I loved to irritate Monica and EJ. You see, both of us were exceptional at determining where the plot was heading and who did what to whom. We would share a knowing glance and one of us would say, "I know ___."

The blank would be what was going to happen next or who the villain was or something that was foreshadowed ever so slightly.

Monica and EJ would either say, "No you don't!!" or "Shut up!" If the former we would blurt out what we knew, or thought we did, and ruin it for them. Occasionally, we were wrong and had to take some heat for it, but with an accuracy rate above seventy five percent, it was well worth it. Our favorite was when they would tell us to shut up.

That simply meant that we could keep needling them, dropping hints, creating misdirection, and generally irritating them until the plot twist was revealed. Man, that was fun. Once Madi was ill, the TV was too loud, the light was too bright, the temperature was too hot or cold, her eyes could not follow the action on the screen. Trying to keep up with the movement would exacerbate her head pain. Movie night disappeared.

Madi loved to learn. She would soak up new information like a sponge. In school, she was forced to take an Anatomy class in a cadaver lab. She was dreading it. She even made her mom go to the first lab with her.

The first lab consisted of the female instructor introducing a cadaver to the students. As the instructor revealed the cadaver, she asked if anyone wanted to touch a heart.

Madi raised her hand walked up to the table, separated the skin, removed the breast plate, reached in, and removed the heart with her hands. She was hooked. She decided right then and there she wanted to be a pediatric neurosurgeon.

Madi and EJ

More than anything, Madi loved her family. She loved to be with her brother. They were inseparable. She loved it when he would come to her softball games and hang out with the team. Fairly sure he liked it too. She loved going to his hockey games, cheering for him when he made a great pass, scored a goal, or slammed another player to the ground. The love she had for him was boundless. She told him she would always take care of him and, if necessary, she would step in front of a bullet for him. She is still making good on her promise today.

Madi and Mom

She cherished the time she spent with her mother. In the car after school, on the way to practice, going to doctors' appointments were some of the most special times they had together. The two of them would talk and laugh about life, love and plans for her future. She loved our home and wanted to raise her family here. When they were both sick at the same time, Monica always found a way to take care of Madi. Regardless of how Monica felt, Madi was her priority and nothing would prevent her from taking care of her little girl. Madi always took the time and made the effort to thank her mom and let her know she loved her. Watching them together increased my love for each of them.

Madi and Daddy

The time she spent with her Coach/Daddy were among the most special. There is a certain bond between a Dad and his daughter. With us it went beyond that. Not only was I her Daddy, her protector and biggest fan, I was her coach. Too often the relationship of coach-child is fraught with favoritism. Not with us. In fact, parents of her teammates would often ask if Madi could ride home with them after games. They were afraid the intensity of our battlefield relationship would spillover to real life. They were constantly amazed at how Madi and I could operate as both coach-player and father-daughter. Madi explained it best when years later she told her mom, "I miss my coach. I know as a Daddy he loves me and will do anything to take care of me. He will run through any wall if he thinks the answer is on the other side. But I need my coach, too. I miss him pushing me, teaching me, challenging me, making me better. I love that about him and wish we could have it back."

CHAPTER EIGHT

Partial Answers and Apathy

There would be glimmers of hope. Small windows that would occasionally open to allow Madi and us to feel "normal" again. They never lasted for long.

There were many more disappointing trips to doctors, specialists, and hospitals that ended in a similar fashion as the visit to the Level 1 Trauma Center. Concerned doctors and nurses fawning over Madi, offering hope they would be the one to finally offer the answers we so desperately wanted. At best, they would offer a singular diagnosis that could not possibly explain the constant pain, fatigue, brain fog, and degradation of her motor skills. At worst, they would tell us they could find nothing wrong.

Each doctor seemed to find something wrong and sent her on for more poking and prodding by specialists or colleagues they felt may be able to dig a bit deeper and find the link between the plethora of diagnoses.

Cardiologist – Postural Orthostatic Tachycardia Syndrome (POTS) – Madi had a resting heart rate of over 120 bpm. Typically, this is most prevalent when moving from a laying to a sitting or standing position and the blood return to the heart is excessively reduced causing dizziness and fainting. Madi suffered from this continually.

Gynecologist – Polycystic Ovarian Syndrome – (PCOS) – PCOS causes irregular or no periods, acne, obesity, and excessive hair growth. In the forty-five days following the visit to the Level 1 Trauma Center, Madi left her bedroom exactly three times. She slept 20 hours per day, ate almost nothing and gained forty-five pounds. On one occasion she went over eleven months without a single period and had to have a surgery to remove excess eggs from around her ovaries. On another, she needed surgery after months long bleeding left her severely weak, anemic and at risk of bleeding out if it was not stopped.

Infertility Specialist – Premature Menopause – This typically strikes women between the ages of 40 and 45. Madi was 17 when she received her diagnosis. She had severe issues with regulating the temperature of her body. She would live at the extremes but never in homeostasis. Often, given her 120 bpm heart rate, she was over heated. Even with the thermostat at 63 in our home, she would sleep on four or five ice packs. Madi always loved children. To know she would never be able to have children of her own was hard on her psyche.

Gastroenterologist – Gastroparesis - This is a stomach disorder that affects the stomach muscles and prevents proper stomach emptying. This impacts digestion and is often caused by damage to the nerves that controls stomach muscles. Gastroparesis is rare. Only about 200,000 cases occur per year in the US. There is no cure.

Renal Specialist – Interstitial cystitis – This is chronic pain that affects the bladder. It is extremely painful and is associated with frequent urinary tract infections, overactive bladder, depression, and a lower quality of life. Only .5% of people in the US are diagnosed with this. There is no cure.

Rheumatologist – Auto-Immune Disease – There are over 100 different types of Autoimmune Disease. The doctors were not able to pare Madi's problems to a specific diagnosis. Madi showed signs of celiac, inflammatory bowel, and Graves' diseases, among others. All more typical in people two to three times Madi's age.

Pediatric Hematologist/Oncologist – Chronic Anemia - When your body stops producing enough new blood cells or the red blood cells are being destroyed at a higher than normal rate. Your body becomes fatigued, more prone to infection and uncontrolled bleeding, like nosebleeds. This was one of the first diagnoses that Madi received.

Pain Management – Chronic Pain – Imagine, with all the things going on in Madi's body she would have chronic pain. Her nerves were constantly on fire and her joints ached with every move. Her head would go from a dull achy pain to sharp extreme pain at any minute for any reason. Initially Madi underwent a three-day hospital stay where she was put in a Propofol coma. It was an attempt to shut down and restart her brain. It had short term benefits, but nothing that could be considered successful. After that, Madi would periodically undergo Ketamine infusions. Each time, she would be hooked up to an IV for four hours. The goal was to interrupt and reset the pain signals. Reality was that at least during the four hours in the chair, Madi would have no pain. Madi also received special Ketamine gummies to be used when she was at home. They would dull the pain a bit, but not much more.

Many of the visits to the doctor, specialist or hospital were not unlike the visits that you or your loved ones may have.

There is one day, however, that I hope and pray none of you ever have to endure. It came at a time when we were at a low point in terms of our hope. More importantly, it was a day where the absolute and total disinterest of the members of the medical community was on full display.

Madi was in intense pain most of the day. I came home from work, went into her cold dark room to talk to her. She looked at me with a pale blank face.

I said, "Hi Baby, are you doing okay?"

She looked at me as if it were the first time she had laid eyes on me. She tried to speak but what came out was gibberish. She was either having a seizure or stroke right before my eyes. I carried Madi to the car yelling for Monica to get her things and open the door. The nearest hospital was the one where Monica's neurosurgeon had privileges. We headed straight there. Madi had come out of the daze just enough to know where she was as we pulled into the parking lot.

We went through the ER ritual and were put in a room quickly. During the initial evaluation we shared the story of the gibberish, the pale cold face, and the vacant eyes with the doctor. When she asked Madi if she remembered anything, Madi was slow to respond and told the doctor she did not. Her words came haltingly and were labored. An MRI showed that Madi had unexplainable lesions on her brain. They moved her to a room down the hall tucked into the corner designed for longer term observation. It seemed to be their way of admitting her without really admitting her.

Once tucked away in the corner, the care and concern of most around us disappeared. The only person that took an interest was a nurse who would check on us regularly.

We had just been told that our daughter had lesions on her brain, were put in a dark corner of the hospital and did not see the doctor again until she was preparing to go off shift the next morning.

She entered the room to tell us the lesions did not pose a long-term threat so Madi needed to be released before the shift change.

Incredulous, we were slow to gather Madi's things and leave. The nurse who had been checking on us through the night came in one last time. She looked behind her as she slowly walked up to us.

She reached out her hand and quietly said, "I can get in a lot of trouble for this, but your daughter is in serious condition. Here is a copy of the MRI. Please take her to another hospital and get her the help she needs."

We were blown away. The nurse was letting us know our fears were well founded and Madi did not receive proper care. We could not believe our ears.

It was early morning and Madi's Neurologist opened in forty-five minutes. We went to a drive through and had breakfast as Madi lay in the back curled up in a ball. We called and were immediately connected to the Physician's Assistant. She had been on call that night, and unbeknown to us the ER doctor had reached out to her. The PA said she was awaiting results from specific tests she asked be run.

"What tests?" we asked.

The PA rattled off four or five different tests that she requested be done based on the results of the MRI and Madi's symptoms. None of them had been done.

We found out that while the neurosurgeon was based at that hospital, the neurologist did not have admitting privileges there. As a result, the ER doctor disregarded the PA's requests.

She instructed us to head straight to the second hospital where the neurologist did have privileges. The PA would call ahead and arrange a direct admit so we would not waste more time in the ER.

As a PA, there are a fair number of things that she could do. What she could not do was request a direct admit at a hospital. Unfortunately for us, it was a Friday and the PA was covering for the neurologist who was out of town.

The ER doctor at the second hospital was amazing. He was empathetic, listened to Madi's story, and asked all of us questions to attempt to understand what could possibly be happening. He actually consulted with the PA and together they devised a care plan.

The plan could only be carried out if Madi was admitted to the hospital, so he helped arrange for her to be moved to the proper floor for stroke patients. With last night's experience still fresh in our minds, we wanted to be sure to not leave anything to chance. We spoke to the PA and ER doctor at length about the plan. We were assured that Madi would not receive the same lack of care she had the night prior. We felt at peace as if a weight had been lifted and hope restored. Upon arriving at the room, Madi began to have serious stroke symptoms again. Her face drooped, her words would not come out and her right side went numb. The attending nurse was great and helped Madi and us through a very scary time.

"Good thing we are in the right place," we thought to ourselves.

Because the Hospitalist had not yet seen Madi, she was not connected to the proper equipment to record evidence of her episode.

As he eventually strolled into the room, hands in his pockets, stern look on his face, his first words to us were, "You aren't going to like me very much."

Excuse me! I have seen some crappy bedside manners in my time, but this was over the top.

"Why is that?" I asked.

"I don't take orders from a PA or an ER doctor and I am not going to run any of the tests they are requesting," he stated ever so clearly and ever so condescendingly. Even the nurses looked at him in disbelief.

Except for one nurse that was just finishing hanging a saline bag.

"I wouldn't either," she muttered under her breath as she passed between Madi's bed and us, "She just needs to put down the fork and step away from the table."

That was the last straw. I snapped.

"What did you say?" I screamed out loud.

"Me?" the nurse replied sarcastically.

"Yes, you!" I went off on her. "What kind of comment is that? Put down the fork? You have no idea what she has endured over the last four years. You know nothing about her or us. You look at us and yes, we are the *fat* family, I get it. I am 5' 10" and 250 pounds, she is 5'5" and 160, Madi is 5'3" and 165. What you do not know is that when I was your age, I was a cheerleader tossing little girls like you in the air and doing back handsprings and flips down the football field. She was a dancer and athletic trainer. Now both of us are cancer survivors. My wife has beaten it twice! And this little girl in the bed. Up until recently she was an elite athlete being recruited by Division 1 schools. Her illness has stolen all of that from her and you tell her to put down the fork. How dare you!"

You could have heard a pin drop in that entire wing of the hospital. I was furious. You want to come at me for anything, fine, bring it on. You go after my baby girl when she has just endured the worst night of her life and lay helpless in bed. No ma'am. That is not going to happen.

Looking at the doctor, I let him know I did not want that nurse anywhere near us. I also realized that he was not going to be swayed by anything he did not experience personally.

I had to shift gears quickly. "I know you weren't here when Madi was in the throes of her episode, but your nurses were. They can tell you what happened. I am sure if you talk to them, they can help you decide the best course of action."

They went away to discuss it and we were left to calm down. Madi squeezed my hand, looked into my eyes and without speaking a word said, "Thank you Daddy, I love you."

The doctor returned, went to Madi, and gave her a standard exam. He turned to us and told us a nurse would come and examine Madi for evidence of stroke. "Evidence of a stroke", I said to myself. "Is the fact the right side of her face is drooping not enough of a sign?"

Instead I asked, "What about a neurology consult?"

"We won't be talking about that," he said.

There are tests showing brain lesions, the nurses have witnessed at least one stroke first-hand and he has already made up his mind a neurology consult was not necessary? This was going nowhere fast.

The nurse came and did the exam. She mentioned she felt there was a significant variation between the left and the right side of Madi's face. However, she got all the test questions correct so her brain was functioning. Barely, the questions were such that a third grader of moderate intelligence would pass. Madi was a Dean's List kind of student, and it took her several minutes to answer each one. I lowered my head and prayed that God would give me the strength to endure the idiocy.

The doctor came in and informed us they would keep her on fluids for another hour or two, but when that was done, she would be sent home.

I looked him in the eye, listed off five or six of Madi's health issues and asked him, "If this was your daughter what would you do?"

As long as I live, I will never forget his answer.

"Sir, that is above my pay grade. I have no idea how to solve all those issues. If you come to me with a broken arm, I can cast it and send you on your way. I am not here to solve all her medical conditions. I am here to make sure she is not in imminent threat of death and I don't believe she is at this time."

"Am I not in a hospital? Are there not doctors on staff who are paid for patient care? If not here, where are we going to find that kind of help," I asked.

"You are obviously educated. I suggest that you hire your own team of doctors and have them study her as a collective. I cannot and will not use the resources of this hospital to solve your personal problems," the doctor answered coldly.

It seems inconceivable now that any medical "*professional*" would act that way, say those things, and keep his job. It is possibly even more inconceivable that I did not end up in handcuffs. Fortunately for him, my full attention was devoted to Madi and finding help for her.

Madi had seen well over a hundred doctors and had been in over seven hospitals by that time. I called every doctor and every hospital searching for that elusive answer. Most calls were dead ends. One however, yielded a possible solution.

We learned there was a world-renowned headache clinic that, if qualified and accepted, Madi would travel the 1,300 miles to live in the hospital. For thirty days she would be reviewed by all sorts of

specialists and experts in the field. She applied
and was accepted. With a great deal of excitement
and hope, Madi and I boarded a plane and off we
went. Her room was beautiful. The facility was
great. It was a full-service hospital with a floor
specifically for people with headaches of all
different kinds. The staff was great, the doctors
skilled and empathetic. The treatments were
wide and varied and Madi tried them all.

Due to the number of doctors and treatments
involved, the morning consultations were critical.
They would happen any time between 5:00-
9:00AM. Madi's failing memory would not allow
her to retain all of the details. We needed a plan.

After the first day, I bought a twin sized blow up
bed and slept on it next to Madi's bed for the
remainder of the month. There we were, fighting
the good fight together. Ordering food from some
great local restaurants and sharing this journey
together. If she were not held hostage in a
hospital and this were a daddy and daughter
outing, it would have been amazing. As it was, we
cherished the time together.

I could never have been as good a patient as Madi. Always positive, always finding a way to think the next test, the next exercise would be the one that would finally allow her to turn the corner. After thirty days, things were not any better, no answers were provided, and we were sent on our way once again.

If the top headache clinic in the country could not help us, it seemed obvious to us and the staff we were not dealing with any kind of "headache". This head pain was being caused by something no one had ever seen, could not or would not identify. Perhaps they did not want to. Perhaps the cause, if identified, would have implications far beyond healing my daughter.

CHAPTER NINE

The Point of No Return

There comes a point where you realize finding the cause and fixing the problem is not realistic. I call it *the point of no return*. You are no longer trying to return to what once was. You are simply working to minimize what is and make the best of it.

We started to look at non-related medical specialties and Eastern medicine. In these disciplines, Madi actually found some relief.

We were introduced to Eastern medicine at the headache clinic late in her visit. The last week of her time there she received several treatments. While not life changing, they provided some relief. When we returned home, we decided to investigate local options to continue that relief.

Eastern medicine worked on balancing her Yin and Yang. She received a combination of treatments consisting of acupuncture, acupressure, Eastern medicine, and therapies. Through these, Madi learned how to reduce her pain when it would spike. It allowed her a small amount of comfort if nothing else.

There was also emerging evidence from the plastic surgery world. It showed a possible correlation between certain procedures and a reduction in migraine headaches.

Without direct evidence and the requisite studies, the procedure was still considered experimental by the vast majority of hospitals and insurance companies. However, we found a doctor who was well versed in the procedure having received specialized training from the pre-eminent expert in the field. He was willing to meet with us.

Madi would undergo nerve decompression surgery. Each of nerves in her forehead and temple would be involved. As we understood it at the time, the nerves sit in pod like structure. The pod can get inflamed to the point that the nerve is constantly compressed and continually sends pain signals to the brain. The procedure allowed the surgeon to remove each nerve from its pod, clean out the pod by removing inflammation, excess tissue or debris and replacing the nerve in a more comfortable and appropriate position. Thus, reducing or eliminating the pain signals.

After a four-hour surgery, Madi was moved to a room for observation and recovery. Initially, there was a good amount of surgical pain so it was difficult to determine if the surgery could be considered a success. A few weeks later, Madi said the pain in her forehead had been reduced from a constant 6-7 on the pain scale to a 2-3. She could live with that. Her temple received slightly less relief. Since we were in a management phase at this point, we considered the surgery a success.

Gradually over time, the pain increased. It was apparent that we needed to revisit the procedure.

Since the initial procedure, the surgeon had refined his techniques. Most critical for Madi was that he had improved his procedure on the nerve beds in the temple. Examinations were done, tests were run, and we scheduled a second surgery.

The surgeon reviewed his plan with us in pre-op. He would do most of the work arthroscopically so scarring would be minimal. In the unlikely event he would need to use an incision, he wanted our approval to do so. We agreed. He had our approval for anything that was required.

Sitting in the waiting room time was dragging on. Those around me came and went. By 4:30 pm I was alone in the waiting room. As several more hours passed, the nurse would come out and say things were going well, it would just be a bit longer.

Finally, the doctor came out just before 9:00 pm. He let me know he was not able to do any of the nerves according to the original plan. Incisions were made for each nerve. The condition of the nerves required not just decompression but total removal. He did not come out personally during the procedure because her nerves were such he had to dig through what I understood to be thick calcification to even get to the nerves. He was incredibly busy and focused.

The nerves were so hardened all the instruments he used had been bent or broken during the procedure. He could barely straighten out his hands from the strain caused by carving out Madi's nerves over ten plus hours. The surgery was so intense she would be admitted into the ICU for constant supervision rather than the typical post-op. When Madi left the hospital the next day, she did so as one of very few people in the country to have all the nerves in her forehead and temple completely removed.

Recovery was brutal. Swelling, bruising, seeping wounds needed constant attention. Madi said it was not anything compared to the spinal taps so many years ago.

One would think that without nerves in the forehead and temple, there would be no opportunity for head pain. One would be wrong. Yes, the pain was reduced across the board to a consistent 3 out of 10, but not erased. It would still spike to a 10 every so often and render her incapacitated, but the frequency was reduced.

We were firmly in the management stage and may have found the answer allowing Madi to return to a semblance of life. Appearances can be deceiving.

CHAPTER 10

A Small Respite and a Purpose

The removal of Madi's nerves, while not a cure, did allow her to do some of the things she had previously loved and lost. She was able to return to reading. Not at the level she was used to, but she was thrilled to be able to see her friends at the library again.

We started to have a family movie night again and Madi made it through most of them. Mind you, we live in South Texas and EJ and I were forced to wear winter pajamas and cover up with two to three blankets each. Our thermostat was very rarely set above 63 degrees. The only reason Madi allowed 63 was because EJ's hockey number was 63. Even in her madness, there was always a method.

Most importantly for Madi, she was able to do something she had always longed to do. She began a blog, *(In)Sane in Chronic Pain.*

She was determined to help other Spoonies that suffered like she did. Not familiar with Spoonies? Let me enlighten you.

Spoon theory is a metaphor for those with disability or medical issues to describe the amount of mental and physical energy available for everyday life. Christine Miserandino coined the term in her 2003 essay, "The Spoon Theory". The spoon is the physical representation of an amount of energy.

Every task has a given number of spoons that are required to complete that task. Every Spoonie has a limited number of spoons to spend that day. Decisions must be made on how to spend each valuable spoon. Things that "normies" take for granted must be carefully considered by a spoonie. It takes careful planning and prioritizing for a spoonie to make it through the day.

Do you think about how taking a shower will impact your day? Probably not. Spoonies do. It may take three spoons for a shower. If a spoonie starts with ten, that is 30% of the day's energy. Getting dressed? Costs you a spoon. Breakfast? There is another one. Driving yourself to an appointment is two more. Having someone take you is only one. Better get a ride. That is 60% of your energy and you have not even gotten to the doctor yet. The life of a spoonie is complicated and exhausting. Anything to make it better or easier is a Godsend.

Madi wanted to be that for others. Her blog was a way to share her experiences and short cuts. She could reach out to other spoonies and learn from them. She could encourage others.

Her blog began, "I've spent almost 2000 days in pain and I've somehow managed to get through every single one. I am not an expert, but I sure can run with the big dogs. So whether you're here just to feel like you're not alone, because someone in your life is chronically ill, or you just want to see what it's like to have chronic pain, buckle up, because that is what this whole blog is for."

She started her blog on December 25, 2016. Her first blog was her origin story, which I must admit she was able to communicate more concisely than I have. That same day, she penned the following blog:

No Man Left Behind

"No man left behind," they say. Saying it over and over and over until it is engrained into the fabric of our being. So, from a young age we are programmed to think our peers will adhere to that policy. Most of the time they do. Until you get sick and are confined to a bed almost 24 hours a day. If you are lucky you will have people who will support you through it all, but that is not what I am talking about.

When you are chronically ill to the point I previously mentioned, your life stops: you are "stuck". However, the world still spins without you. And this can lead to a depressive state where one feels completely left behind. It is not your friend's fault that they get to have a normal college experience. It is not your cousins' fault that they got married, it is not your friend's fault that your best friend had a baby, they are just living their lives.

And from personal experience: It really hurts. There is no sugar coating the fact that someone out there is living a life that we wish we could live, and I am guilty of it, too. I wish that I could go out without weighing the consequences of exerting my energy. I wish I could go to a concert so loud my ears ring days after, but I can't. I must count my spoons every day and dole them out with the precision of a sharpshooter because I am limited.

At first, I was bitter. How come my best friend got to go to college? How come my teammate got the scholarship when she did not do the work? I shut them out, shut down and retreated into myself, but then I realized there is another option:

I can have a life. For normal people this may hardly seem as though it is a groundbreaking idea, but for someone with chronic illness it seems like a fairytale. Here is a short list of tips on how to have a life when you have a debilitating illness:

1) Skype with friends
   You do not have to be physically present to stay connected. You can use Skype, Facetime or any type of technology that lets you converse with your friends without ever leaving your bed.
2) Play online games
   Remember Words with Friends or Draw Something? Bring it back in style. Play any game on your phone, gaming console or computer where you can connect to your friends or family and get some healthy competition going.
3) Come out of your room
   When you have severe chronic pain all you want to do is stay curled up in bed. Do not! Go sit on the couch and watch TV with your family. Being surrounded by people that love you for at least a bit will make you feel

a part of something. And you can never underestimate the importance of that.

4) Make sure to know your limit
   When making plans, if you know all you can do is go to a movie, then only go to the movie. Do not get guilt tripped past your limit because I promise you will most definitely pay for it later.
   Good Luck out there!!

~~ Madi Ferris

From the very first entry, she wanted to help people. Whether to understand the plight of a spoonie or for a spoonie to not feel isolated and alone. Some of the titles of her blog were:

Diary of Spoonie #1: The Holidays
Dealing With Doctors That Don't Believe You
Pain, Isolation, and Therapy
Insurance Sucks
The Danger (and necessity) of saying "I'm fine"
You Look So Well

Every one of then ended with *"Good Luck out There."*

Madi also wanted to offer a perspective other than her own. In March, she asked me for to write a blogpost. She posted it March 11, 2017. It went like this:

"I asked my dad to write a blogpost. I told him to write whatever he wanted.

As always, it turned out amazing and I will now share it with you! Love you, dad!"

CHAPTER ELEVEN

Chronic Pain Kid – A Parent's Perspective

"As a parent our job is quite simple and yet so complex. We are entrusted with the nurturing of a young life, with the responsibility to protect that life from all manner of attacks and help develop that life to its full potential. We must deal with numerous outside opinions and influences from the start, from pacifiers to car seats from cloth to disposable diapers. Every decision seems so important to fulfilling our promise of caring for our child.

Especially with the first child, every decision is debated, analyzed, and cloaked in the veil of having an indelible impact on the entirety of her future. Somehow, we get through it all. The sleepless nights, the colds, coughs, scraped knees, and hurt feelings. Our child grows and develops her personality each and every day. Your hopes and dreams for her future are reshaped and start to morph into her hopes and dreams.

They become shared as you work together to build a base of knowledge, values, and experiences from which to launch those hopes and dreams into orbit and begin turning them into achievable goals and objectives. They take on more importance as they become concrete and plans are made to realize them. They now become real, true attainable possibilities. All the hard work, sweat, and tears are ready to pay off.

You and your child have completed one part of the journey and stand at the doorstep of another. You feel proud of your child for all she has accomplished, confident in the strong base you have provided, yet anxious to see how she continues to develop into a young woman, capable of taking on the world and beating it.

The view from that place was beautiful. The challenges, real and perceived, of the past have been vanquished giving you and she the confidence that future challenges would be as well.

Then one day it all changes. Gradually at first, *Surely, this is just a temporary detour.*

You do as you have in the past. You commit to protecting your child and finding those that can identify the problem and solve it. Then it deepens as you trudge to more and more appointments. More and more specialists, none of which can provide any sense of certainty and only a few that even attempt to give any hope that you can change the current course, get the plans back on track and rejoin the original journey.

Then it happens. You are faced with the one word that appears like the least favorite card in Monopoly, *Go Directly to Jail. Do not pass go. Do not collect $200.* The only difference is that in Monopoly, you have a chance to roll doubles or pay to be released and return to your journey, albeit a bit behind, but with the opportunity to catch up and even win the game.

Chronic - Long Lasting - Constantly Recurring Difficult to Eradicate

No chance to roll doubles. No amount of money can make it go away. Obviously, this is not the worst word you can hear. Terminal, for one, strikes the ultimate fear in the hearts of loved ones and those that face that diagnosis.

My heart and prayers go out to anyone facing a terminal situation. The most significant difference is that *chronic* when used in conjunction with any medical term basically means, "We don't know". It means that there is not a path; well-defined, rustic, over-grown or otherwise, to take. There are no steps to provide any comfort of working toward a solution.

As humans, we are programmed to want to make things better, to fix broken things. Even with our world trending toward planned obsolescence where items that no longer work are simply discarded and replaced with a newer, faster, sleeker model. Thankfully, that is not yet the case with most human life. The problem is, when "chronic" creeps in, there is no fix.

When Monica was diagnosed with cancer at 24, there was a possible fix. When Placenta Previa threatened to rob us our first child, there was a path we could follow. When I joined Monica in the cancer club 18 years later by contracting colon cancer, the fix was more invasive and less certain, but it was there. When a brain tumor tried to rob me of the mother of my children and love of my life a second time, again, there was a fix. A wonderful doctor that could provide no guarantees but a path that if followed was likely to yield positive results. In every one of these situations, we were faced with the very real possibility of tremendous physical pain, mental anguish, and catastrophic loss. We were able to face these head on, implement the plan placed before us with the help of tremendous professionals and commit to overcoming a formidable but known foe.

This time there would be no plan, no professional help. No path to overcome this unknown foe before you. That is when you become:

Hopeless and Helpless
Hope is the engine that drives us forward
The thought that our tomorrow will be better than our
today
Help is the glue that binds us together
The coming together for a common cause that shows our
humanity
Less on its own is simply not as much
A way of illustrating quantity or value
Why then when we pair them does it make such a
monumental shift?

Hopeless is devoid of all hope
Helpless is completely without help.
Normally full of hope and willing to help,
Tonight, we find ourselves at the corner of hopeless and
helpless
Hopeless because every road seems a dead end
Helpless because those in a position to provide
assistance remain aloof
They stand on the side in disbelief as the stories are
told
Of trials and tribulations, of pain and suffering
They lack a fundamental understanding of the paths
that have been walked
They possess a bias that colors their thoughts and
actions and stand in the way of finding a solution
It is a dark corner on which we stand
Lonely, tired, broken and wasted
So much hope to share, so much help to give
All laid to waste at this intersection
A once bright light reduced to barely a flicker
God, help us understand why this path has led us here
We trust you have a reason, a plan.
Please help us to find our way off this dark corner and
back into your light.

At that dark corner, you are forced to choose. Do you simply give in or do you face the challenge head on? You search your heart, your soul, your faith, and your bank account. Then, as you are facing what seems to be an insurmountable challenge, you realize, "We have done this before!"

You look back and realize that while there were plenty of opinions and influencers, YOU raised that child. YOU provided the structure and values that shaped her life. YOU were the one that stayed up with her at night. YOU were the one that wiped her nose and tears away. YOU were the one who bandaged those scraped knees and hurt feelings. YOU are strong and YOU are capable. YOU can and MUST do this. If it is meant to be, it is up to YOU! Failure is not an option. There will be no white flags of surrender. You will battle this foe on its terms. You will leave no stone unturned to find a way if not to overcome the foe, to marginalize it in such a way to allow you and your child to live a meaningful, productive life.

Those hopes and dreams that together you turned into goals and objectives, that she built into attainable possibilities get adjusted or delayed. You now stand together at the doorstep of a journey with a less certain vision. One that requires more strength, more diligence and more intestinal fortitude than you previously thought imaginable.

You take your loved ones by the hand, ask God for guidance and strength, strap on your mental armor, reach for the handle, turn it, and open the door to an amazing journey. One you never anticipated. One that will test your faith, your heart, your strength, and your sanity. One that will also define your character, deepen your relationships, and forge bonds that will never be broken.

CHAPTER TWELVE

A Mother's Love

The following month, she asked her mom to write about what she would tell others. On April 2, 2017, she posted her mother's words.

Advice From My Mom

"We have to live a new life that would not seem possible. But that is not something you need to be Superman to accomplish," Christopher Reeve said in *Nothing is Impossible 2003*.

Madeline asked me what it is like to parent a chronically ill child. It feels like I am a firefighter sometimes. I am ready to tackle new symptoms, run to the ER, the doctor or whatever is needed that day. The first thing chronic illness taught me as a parent was to be flexible.

Chronic comes from the Latin word *chronicus*, meaning lingering and pertaining to time. You quickly learn your schedule does not matter.

I also learned this takes your time, your most precious gift.

I am always asked by friends how we deal with Madi's illness and how we function as a family as a result. Here are some of the tips I have learned:

1) Laminate a medication list. You always need to know what you child has taken that day and when.

2) Let your child rest. Healing is resting. Do not push your child through the pain.

3) Know your child's limits. Frequently on good days, they will want to overdo. They will end up paying for this and it could make them worse.

4)Consider a pet for your child. We have two dogs and they are pure joy to us. They wake up with us late at night and are our constant companions.

5) Consider a nutritionist to help maintain the best diet you can afford.

6) Doctor's appointments are a fact of life. They can take an entire day. Try not to overschedule your child. Madi needs two days to recover from a single appointment.

7) Consider making their bedroom an electronic free zone. Have them rest/read in their room only. Have them watch TV or work on the computer in a family room.

8) Listen to your child daily. Sometimes they just want to talk. Stop and listen.

9) Make time for your friends, too. I know it is hard to leave your child but try to make time. Your child is fighting every day, but you are too.

10) Laughter is the best medicine. Keep your sense of humor.

11) Take care of yourself. If you run yourself ragged you are no good to your child.

12) You are your child's best advocate. Fight for them. Ask a lot of questions in appointments. If the doctor has a terrible bedside manner or does not listen to you or your child, move on. A good doctor is gold.

13) Let people help. Do not always feel like you must do everything.

14) Forgive yourself. Sounds easy, but as parents we want to blame ourselves.

15) Watch positive movies. We try to have a family movie night weekly. It gets everyone together and is one of the few things we can all do together.

16) Stay flexible. It is okay. It does not all have to be done today.

17) Consider Chinese medicine. This has really helped.

18) The best tip is the last: Enjoy every minute of a good day!

Every spoonie knows a good day makes you want to share it on every social media platform available. It is such a joy to feel good.

We had to learn to live a new life with chronic illness. It is not what we planned and as Christopher Reeve said, it would not have seemed possible. We had to grieve the old life. Our home went from the constant noise of softball girls to silence. We used to spend every weekend in a different city for softball or hockey. Madi was going to have her pick of colleges.

The first year of illness is a blur trying to find out what happened and fix it. Then comes that moment when you realize you must hand it over to God and let him handle it. My husband and my family are a great support for me. I have several family members I can dump on any time of day or night. This is invaluable to me. It can be done. You do not have to be Superman. I learned a long time ago to retire my cape. I thought I could do it all. In the end, after you have burned the candle at both ends, you have nothing left.

Anyone that knows me knows I love Amy Grant. She has been my favorite singer for decades. Her song, *Somewhere Down the Road*, captures it best:

"So much pain and no good reason why, you've cried until the tears run dry. And nothing here can make you understand, the one thing that you held so dear is slipping from your hands. And you say, Why, why, why does it go this way? Why, why, why is all you can say.

Somewhere down the road, there will be answers to the questions. Somewhere down the road, though we cannot see it now. Somewhere down the road, you will find mighty arms reaching for you and they will hold the answers at the end of the road."

It is a great song for loss and the need to begin anew. Sometimes we just do not know why. We do not know what our journey will hold.

I ask God daily for the strength to keep walking for *that day.* I also learned I married a hero. A person I can trust to be there at any time and any moment I need him. We are in this together, all in one hundred percent.

It took me a long time to realize to enjoy the moments. I stop and recognize the moments now. I appreciate the times we laugh, and the times Madeline is comfortable. We do not have all the answers, but we will find them together, somewhere down the road."

~~ Monica Ferris

Madi was so proud of her mom. Not only for being able to lend a special perspective to an incredibly challenging topic, but for all the times they sat together talking, crying, or just holding each other.

Those times are invaluable as a family. When you spend so much of your time and effort fighting an unknown foe, you need to know those closest to you will always be your refuge, your sanity, and your peace. Having gone through so much together, we finally felt at a place of balance. Little did we know how short-lived that balance would be.

CHAPTER 13

Loss

May had always been a month for celebration in our family. Our wedding anniversary was on May 14. Mother's Day was on the same day in 2017, as it was the day we were married. My birthday on the 25th and Memorial Day capped off the month.

Things were going well. Madi was managing her pain between a 3 and 7 and our Mother's Day and anniversary celebrations were complete.

That week was a time for rest before things ramped up again, or so we thought.

May 16 was like any other day. I went to work, EJ went to school and Monica and Madi held down the fort. Monica had been in the hospital with a nasty bout of diverticulitis the previous week, so it was nice to have things back to somewhat normal.

When I got home from work, Monica had dinner ready, but it was obvious she had worn herself out. EJ had a good day at school and was busy with homework. Madi was in a good mood having just started a French class at the local library. She was excited to tell me all about it and the people in her class. They were all much older and welcomed her youthful energy and excitement into their class. She was so happy to be learning again.

We had dinner and everyone retreated to their respective corners. Monica went to our bedroom to rest, EJ back to his room to finish homework, and Madi to her room to blog about her day and French class. I sat in the media room watching TV, enjoying some time to relax and not think about anything for a while.

At 8:00PM I went into our room to check on Monica. She had fallen asleep with the TV on. I took her glasses, put them on the nightstand, turned off the television and lights.

EJ finished his homework and came out with me for a bit. He did not stay long as he did not care for my habit of changing channels and watching two or three things at once.

Madi came out just before 9:00 PM. One of the things I was watching was *The Replacements* with Gene Hackman and Keanu Reeves. Believe it or not, that was one of Madi's favorite movies and Keanu one of her favorite actors.

The movie and Keanu's character fit her personality. She liked the idea of a bunch of random ex-footballers getting the chance to show they are a better team than a collection of high-priced prima donnas. She particularly liked Shane Falco. Shane, played by Keanu, was a former college quarterback who famously flamed out in the pros and now made his living scrapping barnacles off other people's boats. Due to a strike, an old unconventional coach, Jimmy McGinty, played by Hackman, wanted Falco as his quarterback. He believed in Shane more than Shane did.

Together, they ultimately proved that the right team with the right objectives, and no ego can become winners.

Funny how art sometimes imitates life, eh? How much did this movie influence Madi? She would not admit it until years later, but when asked to choose a number for softball at the age of eight, she chose 16 because she wanted to be a leader like Shane. As she grew older, she wanted to learn more about Keanu Reeves. She researched his life, learned of his personal struggles, perseverance, humility, and good heart. She was impressed and wanted to emulate him. The number 16 became more than just a way to pay homage to a movie character, it represented an attitude. An attitude of gratitude, humility, and the perseverance not only to overcome her own struggles, but to help others. She wore that number with pride and a purpose.

As she walked toward the room, I clicked over to the movie. It just so happened to be at the point where Shane arrives at training camp. She looks toward the screen, laughs, throws her arm up in front of her face and says, "Dad! No, I am tired, please do not tell me that is on. I want to go to bed." How I wish we would have watched the rest of the movie.

She came in because she wanted her night meds and did not want to wake up her mom. We kept all the meds in a safe in our bedroom. Monica was usually the keeper of the meds. Given all the diagnoses Madi had and the associated medicines with each, it was imperative that meds were tracked and managed. I turned the channel, got up, hugged her, and said, "I know baby, come on, let's get them."

We went to the safe, got the appropriate meds, Madi said, "Thanks Daddy, love you." And we went our separate ways. Madi to her room, me back to the media room.

At 10:00 PM, my shows ended. I started to get up to go to bed. As I did, I grabbed the remote and the channel changed to the *Golf Channel* and *Feherty*. I like his show and enjoy a good laugh but would not call myself a hard-core viewer. Stephen Curry was his guest. I am not an NBA guy, but Stephen fits the underdog role that Madi and I like so much. I oddly decided to invest an hour of my life to hear his story.

When the show ended, I locked doors, turned out lights and headed for the bedroom. Entering the room, I noticed our bathroom door closed and light on with Monica still asleep. Madi had decided to take a bath to soothe her nerves, which, while inconvenient for me, was not unusual.

What was unusual was my silence. I said nothing. Typically, I would say, "Come on Madi. Really?" or something to jab her a bit.

All I did was get irritated that I could not use my own toilet and went next door to hers. As I approached the toilet, I noticed something odd. It had not been flushed.

Getting more irritated by the minute, I tried to flush it, but it did not work. I fixed the toilet, flushed it, finished what I came for and made sure it worked a second time.

Completely angry by now, I was ready to let Madi have it. Not only could I not use my own toilet in my own bedroom before bed, but I had to fix a toilet that she did not tell me was broken before I could us it.

I entered my bedroom intent on blasting Madi from the door of our bathroom. As I took my second step in the room, something physically stopped me from taking a third step. "Not now," a voice said.

"What? What do you mean not now?" I said to the voice under my breath.

"Now is not the time. I will take care of her." the voice said, "Go to bed."

I turn to the bed on my right, do not say a word, lay down and go to bed.

Less than an hour later, I hear a blood curdling scream.

"MADELINE! OH MY GOD!! CALL 911!!!"

Monica had gotten up, walked into the bathroom and saw Madi at the bottom of our tub. I flew from the bed into the bathroom. There was the body of my little girl, under the water in the fetal position hands together as if she were praying.

Everything after that was absolute chaos. EJ came running from his room, grabbed the phone, and called 911. Monica screaming, I reach in and try to pull her out of the tub. Her skin feels like a rubber wet suit. EJ helps me get her the rest of the way out and I begin CPR.

"Come on baby, Come back. Come on, you can do it.... Come on Madi, fight, you got this. Find your way back, baby, we are here, find your way back!!!", I implore.

EMS arrives and takes over. Monica, EJ and I gather in the living room and huddle to pray for a miracle. Police show up and ask all kinds of questions. They want all the meds Madi was taking. They want to know what happened that day. They want to search her computer, her phone. EMS comes out and tells me she is gone. They need to call the judge. I ask to see her one more time. Monica and EJ do not want to. I must. I am her Daddy, dammit. I need to.

EMS finally agrees and takes me back to the bathroom. Wires and pads attached to her. Equipment and used supplies on the ground. Madi laying there on the cold ceramic, bloated and blue. I lay down next to her trying to hold back the tears but unable.

"Madi, you deserved so much better. This was not the way it was supposed to go. I love you so much. I am so sorry I failed you. I love you," I say as I reach over to kiss her one last time. My baby is dead. This would be the last time I would ever see her.

Truthfully, the last time I really saw her was when she hugged me and told me she loved me before going to bed.

The body we saw in the water, that I dragged out and gave CPR, that the EMS worked on was not our Madi.   That body was simply the vessel carrying her soul.

Monica would later tell me the reason she woke was the feeling of Madi's warm hand rubbing her back gently in a circle, just the way Madi always woke her when she needed her help.   There was no earthly reason Monica should have been awakened. She had taken a sleeping pill earlier. It usually kept her out for eight to ten hours. When Monica's eyes opened, Madi was not standing there and the bathroom light was on with the door closed. She immediately knew something was wrong.

It was evident to both of us from the moment we laid eyes on Madi in the water, she was already gone. The voice was right. God had taken care of her and relieved her pain.

So Many Emotions

Over the next few days, the flood of sentiments was overwhelming. My job as the head of the family was to keep everything together and be the solid rock foundation that others could lean on. I did the best I could, but EJ was my rock.

In reality, I was a mess. Many people fear death. I never really have. My emotion around it has always been more hatred than fear. Now my feelings were all over the place. The only way I could deal with them was to write from the heart.

The Night Her Eyes Closed Forever

May 16, 2017. That was the night she closed her eyes forever. Big beautiful expressive brown eyes that took in the world around her with wonder and excitement. Now they would never see how her little brother would grow up, how her parents would grow old together, or see how her own life would play out.

Instead of seeing how she would overcome all the challenges placed before her over the past years and watch how her experiences, her toughness, and her determination would inspire others to believe anything was possible, she closed her eyes forever.

As a young girl, those eyes captured the imagination of everyone around her. How could her eyes see and understand so much for such a young child? How could they express her emotions with such depth and sincerity? How could they cut through so much of the clutter surrounding our lives?

As she grew into a young lady those eyes saw so much more. They saw a future full of promise and opportunity. There were no goals so lofty her eyes could not see. There were no horizons that appeared too far away. Life was full of possibilities. She saw her life as one that would help others. She saw how others were misunderstood or mistreated and made it her mission to right those wrongs. Her eyes always saw the best in people. She wanted the rest of the world to see what she saw.

Things changed for her along the way. Her once laser focus became cloudy. Her quick reflexes and reactions slowed as pain took over. Slight at first, it began to build until it overtook her every moment and every thought. Unrelenting head pain beyond imagination. Nerve pain ravaged her body without reason or warning.

Every system in her body was impacted by a riddle without a clue that would dull her sparkling eyes to an empty stare. While there were occasional sparks of those bright beautiful eyes over the last few years, they were nothing more than fleeting moments of what had been and a tease of what we hoped could be again. Regrettably, it was not to be.

I pray that when she closed her eyes to us forever, they were opened to the most beautiful sight any of us will ever see. I pray her big beautiful brown eyes were restored to see the glory of the Lord our God. I pray that her eyes are once again experiencing the wonder around her. I know her heart is still reaching out to those grieving her loss telling them she has been restored to the happy carefree Madi of her youth, laughing, smiling, and giggling. Making those around her rejoice in her presence in her energy and her purity of heart.

On the night she closed her eyes forever, they were opened again.

CHAPTER 14

Day One of the Rest of Our Lives

Today is the first day of our new lives. When I awoke the sounds were vaguely familiar but somehow different. The birds' chirping was somehow slower and less joyful. The planes going overhead were monotonous and plodding rather than sharp and focused.

The sounds of the home were hollow. Acorns falling from trees and hitting the roof, the air conditioning turning on, the wind against the windows and the dogs patrolling the halls were all there. They were just a bit off balance and time. Maybe that is our new normal.

Life without Madi will have a different tone, a different tenor, a different pace. She added life. She added a sharpness to everything she did or touched. Sometimes annoyingly so, but always with purpose and always with energy. We will never replace her presence. We will miss her every minute of every day. Somehow, we must find a way to live our lives without her. We must find it in ourselves and each other to sharpen our senses, rededicate our efforts, and live with a purpose.

For so long she was our purpose. Initially as our first child, a challenge and honor from God to guide and develop. Then more recently as our wounded one. Her body invaded by pains and problems no one could explain or relieve. She became a cause unto herself, a never-ending quest for answers. Her life drove ours. She gave it purpose and direction. Our compass is gone, our goal erased, our soundtrack has changed.

This is the first day of our new life and we are lost. God, please help us find our way in this new life as you celebrate Madi's new life with you. You definitely got the better end of the deal.

The Pain is Gone and It Hurts Like Hell

Last evening our beautiful daughter Madeline joined her true Father in heaven.
After fighting a monster for more than four years, she did not succumb to it. She slipped ever so slowly into a deep sleep while soothing her nerves in a warm tub. She was fighting it to the end. She was finding ways to overcome it or render it neutral. Her pain is gone. Her life now eternal.

The pain she leaves behind is immense. The people she touched forever changed. Her mother, brother and I left to carry on without her by our side.

The hole left in our family and in our hearts will never fully heal. The pain she endured passed on to us in the form of guilt, sadness, despair, and longing. We share that burden. It is one we carry always and everywhere. It may fade over time but will never disappear.

Madi carried her pain for the past six years. It had to be more unimaginable than I ever realized. Pain 24/7/365 keeping her in bed on most days. Pain occasionally subsiding enough to tease her into trying to live the life of a "normie" only to come raging back to knock her further down than before and remind her of her illness.

The crazy thing is no one could tell us what the illness was. They could only say, "Not really sure, but let's see if this work," only to give her more medicine or a higher dosage.

Ultimately, I believe that to have been her undoing. A mysterious set of unexplained medical challenges addressed with medication that did not really work followed by the big guns throwing her for a loop. Last night that loop put her at the bottom of my tub and at the foot of the Father. Her pain is gone. Ours is only beginning and it hurts like hell.

The End of Day One

Day one is coming to a close. Each hour is bringing new experiences, more information, and more peace. Getting out of bed today was the second hardest thing I have ever had to do in my fifty-two years on this earth. You can easily guess the first.

In fact, if we did not have friends call to say they were on the way over we may still be in our cocoon. Thank God for pushing the right buttons there. The first several hours were spent with friends who just recently lost a young son. Through sharing stories, we opened up, they opened up, and some combined healing ensued.

While there are significant differences in our experiences, the similarities and emotions are far more common. We learned also that a penny in a vase of tulips will allow droopy unopened tulips to firm up, open, and be quite beautiful. Something about the copper. Are pennies still made of copper? Wonder if Mom knows the trick. She loves tulips.

It is strange the things you talk about when minds are jumbled and emotions rambling.

Life Limps Forward

We were able to leave the house today. A quick trip, a small trip, but an important one. We had a nice lunch, Monica, and I. EJ went to school for lunch with friends and did some normal kid stuff. He is amazing.

We also got a call from the Judge. The Autopsy has been completed. While we do not know a whole lot more, we do know drowning was a factor, (really?). Until toxicology comes back in six to ten weeks, they will not provide us with a final determination.

The bigger news is they did investigate her brain as I asked and found significant issues in Madi's frontal lobe, something not present in a "normal" brain. They are non-committal about the cause and hopefully we will learn more when we get the full report. It could have been due to her surgeries or something else. We definitely have our suspicions.

I also learned drowning is not the long horrible death I once thought. It is actually one of the quickest ways to go. It only takes six to eleven seconds to drown and there is at least one tub drowning death every day of the year. I never would have guessed.

Things are still a struggle and will be for a long time. The peace of knowing Madi is no longer in pain, and her daily struggle is over is really helping. Getting confirmation that she likely did not suffer provides even more comfort.

Monica still feels the weight of her loss. EJ continues to show he is wise beyond his years. Together we are guiding each other, helping each other to find a new normal. It is strained, it is highly uncomfortable, but it is on its way.

The support from family and friends has been amazing. Everyone wants to lift us up, to love and help us. Help.... it is kind of the tough thing. Everyone wants to help.

"Anything you need, just ask," or "What can we do?" Other variations are offered from all angles.

The challenge is... I do not know what we need, what we want from them. This is a highly personal time. Even having our closest friends and family help seems like dereliction of duty. Madi was our daughter. I need to be involved in the arrangements. I want to write the obituary. I want to control the service. Ok, so maybe I do know what I want and need. But the point is those are not things with which I need or want help.

There are so many things I do need. Know a good maid that can work miracles? Have a tree trimmer to get on our roof and stop the darn branch from rubbing against the fan sounding like our old bicycle wheels with playing cards? How about a rake and a truckload of bags to get rid of all these friggin' leaves? Maybe a truck to take all the crap we have accumulated in weird places in our house to the goodwill or dump?

We absolutely need all those things, but that is not what people want to do and probably are not reasonable asks. Food seems to be a priority for people helping you grieve. Nice and kind, but appetite is not high on my list at the moment.

I love people. I love seeing so many people want to *do something.* I am humbled by some of the people I have heard from and see on the dinner calendar. I am amazed at the people who have heard the news and are reaching out to others we know. I am stunned at the out-pouring of well-wishers and helping hands. There are so many I need to tell thank you. You have no idea how blessed you are or how many people you or your family has touched until times like this. Madi was a joy to so many people.

My mind goes back to so many times at the ball fields, at school, on the playground, at the pool and all the kids she loved. She belonged to everyone and made them smile. I bet she has already started a pick-up game in heaven. God would I love to hear Dad's play by play!!

The Best of Me

As a young child, I followed my parents as they taught me about You.

As a little boy, I began to learn more about You through watching my brothers and sisters and following my teachers and friends.

As a teen, I began my own relationship, giving parts of me to You through service.

As a young man through study and prayer, it was clear that the key to knowing You was to give You all of me. I was weak and resisted, only allowing small parts of me to be given. It was my way of pretending to oversee my own life, to be the master of my own destiny, and to chart a course for my life that was of my own making.

The majority of my life continued that way until You blessed me with the most wonderful gift I had ever received. On November 3, 1995, Madeline Nicole entered my life. Nothing would ever be the same. She was my everything from the time I saw her first pout on that glorious day. She was amazing, incredible and she stole the entirety of my heart.

Starting that day, we learned from each other, we loved each other. We became the best and worst of each other. I started to truly learn what it meant to live for another, to fully surrender to something other than myself.

In giving all I had to her, she became the absolute best of me. We continued our story, our lives. As life meandered along, You were a part of it but not through focused dedication. We served You casually and honored You partially. Our service became to ourselves and our needs. We gave You lip service. We tried to live the golden rule and to honor Your Word through the way we lived our lives without truly giving ourselves to You. We both maintained that we were in control of our lives.

On May 16, 2017, that all changed. You proved that any illusion of control we thought we had was just that, an illusion. On that day you did not ask. You were not subtle. On that day, you took the absolute best of me to be with you in Heaven. On that day, I was forced to give you all of me. There is nothing left.

Once again, I am reduced to the understanding of a child. I am trying to accept Your Will was done that day and Madeline is now able to help others as she always desired. She has been restored in Your Presence, and she serves in Your Light.

As I struggle, I trust that she will continually remind you to be patient with me. You already have the best of me.

You Had One Job!

There is a common saying these days...

"You had one job!" It is usually accompanied by a picture of an epic fail where someone with a relatively easy task makes an error so obvious, they likely did not get another chance.

In an earlier writing, I referenced my one job. It was identified as the most simple complicated job ever... to nurture a young life to its full potential. While there will not be any pictures, I have spent the last thirty days trying to come to terms with my most epic fail ever. One from which I will never, ever be able to recover. An *Epic Fail* with such massive implications that numerous lives have been altered forever.

Truth be told, it was a colossal fail developed over several years, only to culminate in one of the most surreal horrifying nights of my life and the end of another. It ended with my one and only daughter, the love of our lives, and the joy of my heart floating lifeless in my own bathtub. A vision I will never get out of my head and, strangely, one I do not want to. It serves as a sobering reminder that I had one job, and I failed.

There are many stages that fathers go though as their daughters grow and mature. Madi and I got to experience less than half of them. We had an amazing start. You could even call it a fairy tale existence. She was absolutely beautiful, with an engaging smile and a dangerous pout from the moment she took her first breath. She was the best of me... and the worst.

It made for some of the most amazingly fun, exciting, and exasperating times I have ever experienced. We laughed together, we cried together, we fought, and we made up. I was her coach and she was my player, in life and in sports. We experienced so many things together through life and sports. We were inseparable, we knew what the other was thinking and how we could help or hurt the other with our actions or words.

Turns out in the end, actions or words were not the most damaging. It was the lack of action, the lack of words. It was the vision of my almost unrecognizable baby lying on the ceramic floor, half covered with a towel, waiting to be placed in a black plastic bag and removed from my life forever.

No more actions, no more words. No more *I love you, Dad.* There will never be a graduation party. There will never be a night spent healing a broken heart for an unrequited love. There will never be a wedding to plan, a father-daughter dance, a grandchild to spoil and hand back to her full of sugar and boundless energy.

All those firsts to which we had to look forward, lay to waste by a mysterious set of medical issues with a cause no one wants to identify and, as a result, could not remedy. Instead, stronger and stronger medicine took my Bubbles farther away every day. She had not been herself for a long time. Her medical issues, resulting depression, and mental struggles tangled my once happy, healthy, athletic, intense daughter into a tired, bed-ridden, pain filled shadow of her former self.

It is here where I began to fail in my one job, to nurture a young life to its fullest potential. Dads are supposed to fix things. Broken dolls, torn ball gloves, custom made beds with *Pooh* designs are all things Dads are expected to repair.

When our kids scrape their knees, we are supposed to bandage them. When they get a cold, we wipe their noses. When we do not know what to do, we take them to the doctor and rely on their schooling and experience to make them better. For almost fifteen years, that is just what we did. It was wonderful.

Losing her is the price I must pay for not doing the one thing I was supposed to do.

I had one job. Now it is over. Madi and I will not get a second chance.

CHAPTER FIFTEEN

How the Heart Goes On

How does the heart go on? At times like this, it seems almost impossible. Your heart has been ripped out, stomped on, put through a shredder and it is supposed to go on?

Yes, it does, and it must. Because the alternative allows the darkness to win. If we let despair overcome us, the life we mourn is lost twice. It is lost upon its own death and again when it dies in our memories.

Madi's life was too vibrant, too full of joy to allow that to happen. Instead, a memorial was planned. One that would celebrate her life in pictures and music. One that would tell the story of a life well lived, cut short by an illness of mysterious origin.

Our friends, Brandi and Pam, oversaw the pictures and music. They put together an amazing representation of Madi's life and those whom she loved. Together we picked specific music that Madi loved that would display her love for God and her vibrant spirit.

We picked one song that we really wanted and added pictures to allow us to use it. In the end, Brandi and I agreed it was not appropriate for the setting and cut out most of it but one small section. We worked until the early morning hours making the pictures fit to the music.

Once we felt we had nailed it, Brandi went home to rest. I went on to some other things.

Before going to bed, I decided to watch the pictorial montage one more time. Needing to know the exact length for the service, I looked through my watery eyes at the bottom of the screen and could not believe it. I broke into heavy tears and lay my head on the table. After I pulled myself together, I looked at the clock. It was 2:13 AM. Was it too late? Would she still be up? I had to call.

The phone rang, Brandi immediately picked up and said, "Did you see?"

I did see and could not believe my eyes. The video was 16:16 on the dot! It was perfect. It was Bubbles.

The memorial was slated to start at 2:00 PM. The church was packed with people and the procession began. There was a short blessing by the preacher and then it was my turn. I prepared a short eulogy of sorts for Madi and had it timed perfectly. Here is how it went:

The Two Madi's
Today, our immediate family, softball, school, hockey, faith families and other friends all come together as one, we are simply Madi's family.
Together, we lift up her life, celebrate her amazing spirit and visualize her infectious smile.
We will share stories, we will laugh, we will cry. We will remember the special little girl, the beautiful young lady, and the fierce competitor with whom we shared too short a time.
She was amazing, she was life changing, she was intense.

136

But did you know there were two Madeline's?
The Young Madi that so many of us remember as joyful,
living life to the fullest, enjoying every moment and
making things better by her sheer presence. Our
Bubbles: engaging, passionate, always smiling, always
laughing
Then there is the other Madi. The one many of you
know about, but likely do not truly know.
The Madi whose entire body had slowly deteriorated for
the past six years and who had lived in constant pain
24/7/365 since February 3, 2013. The Madi that
visited well over 200 doctors with no relief and no
answers. The Madi that was poked and prodded
constantly, tested from head to toe and operated on
numerous times. The Madi that in December became one
of less than a handful of people
in the country to undergo an extreme procedure that
would remove all of the nerves in her forehead.
That Madi was no less determined, no less engaging,
and absolutely no less passionate. She committed
herself to research and dedicated her time to helping
others. She started a blog to share her experiences and
inspire others. To help just one of the 10's of 1,000's
of children and families around the world suffering from
the same complex combinations of supposedly
unexplainable medical problems was her goal. As was
her habit, she over-achieved.
Over the last week, Monica and I have heard from
literally thousands of them from all over the globe.
Sharing their stories of how Madi's words and her story
have impacted them and how they wish
they could join us today.
As was always the case with Madi, we will find a way.
Together with the 1000's of her brothers and sisters in
pain and their families around the world.
We ask that you join us in a moment of silent prayer
at 2:16pm for our #16.

Thank you for sharing this special time and for celebrating Madi.

It was a special gesture to honor Madi and the vision she had for helping others that would allow us to start the healing process and allow our hearts to go on and move to the *after*.

The After

While it is not exactly clear when it starts, the *after* is a time we all face in our lives. There are different things that cause the after: a good friend moves away, a relationship breakup, the loss of a pet, or the loss of a loved one. Our loved one that caused the after is my daughter, Madeline Nicole. On May 16, 2017, Madi went to be with her true Father in Heaven.

Madi was and is the joy of our lives. She was the best part of me and the most amazing parts of her mother, with just enough of the bad to make life interesting. For 16 years, we had a full life and Madi was at the center of it. Between Madi and her brother, EJ, they kept us busy and on our toes. Softball, hockey, church, school, friends; you name it, we were all in. Love, laughter, and great times were around every corner.

Over the next few years, things slowly changed. Then, one fateful day the light of our lives and the joy of our hearts slipped into a catatonic state while taking a bath and below the water into her eternal rest. The pain that she had lived with for five years, the body that had deteriorated, the mind that was confused and frustrated all restored in the Light of the Father as she took her place in Heaven. That was midnight, May 16, 2017.

Somewhere between then and now, May 30, 2017, the after began. I cannot really say when, but I know how. Our baby is gone, and our lives must move on without her. That is the after. That time when you realize the life that you had before will never be yours again and somehow, someway you must find a way to go on. To honor the memories and celebrate the spirit being set free while simultaneously mourning the loss of a beautiful giving and loving young lady.

I cannot know where our after will lead, but I do know this. It will be guided by the loving hand of our amazing Bubbles. Lead the way Madi.

I Had to Lose My Daughter to Get Her Back

Today I got the forms to tell the insurance company how my baby died and to put in a claim for her insurance coverage. It seemed that her life has boiled down to an exercise in bureaucracy.

Then a text came from my wife. She had read some letters that Madi wrote during a particularly dark time in her life. A time when, after the hundreds of doctors, thousands of tests, numerous surgeries and procedures provided no relief, Madi entered a place where hope had vanished, and despair ruled the day. That day was quite a while ago and I give thanks to God we were able to help each other through those times and find a way to move forward and into the light. It did, however, get me thinking.

When Madi died in our tub on May 16, 2017, was that really the end? In a literal sense, the answer is obvious, but if you replay the entire video, the question becomes harder to answer. In fact, I believe it becomes quite the opposite. It was not the end. It was, in a sense, a rebirth, a return to the true Madi. You see, the pain and various medical maladies from which she suffered had taken away my daughter years earlier. When the onslaught began and we fought together, she was still my Madi. The exuberant, positive, laughing, smiling, and tough kid that was going to defeat whatever lay in front of her. And so it was in this fight. Whatever the doctors said, she would do. Whatever they prescribed, she was up for. When they started to run out of answers, she started researching and looking for options on her own.

Then things changed. I do not really know the date, but there was a marked shift in how she, I and her mother somehow moved into a grey zone. Life was present but was not really there. Smiles were happening but were not really sincere. Laughter, once the lifeblood of our family, disappeared. Madi, my beautiful baby girl had faded away. She mostly became a shut in. If not the pain or discomfort, the medicine that was supposed to relieve those relegated her to the life of a hermit. Dark rooms, sunglasses, light clothes, cold temperatures, soft blankets, and popcorn became her life. Rarely did she come out of her room.

Occasionally, we were able to get her to come watch TV with the rest of us. When she did, the TV was too loud, the lights too bright or the food was too spicy for her to stay out with us for too long. There were days that she could try to live the life of a "normie." For several years though, she just existed. Not because of a lack of desire or drive, but because her body was robbed of the energy required to change clothes on a daily basis, much less focus on a formerly bright future.

And so it was for the last few years. We got up, put one foot in front of the other, told ourselves that God had a plan and that the doctors, one of them anyway, would find a way if not to eliminate the challenge at least mitigate it to the point she could have a meaningful life. But there really was not any life. It was a constant fight. A fight to control her pain, her fatigue, her heart, her nerves, her vision, her nausea. A fight to pull her out of the dark coldness of her room and into the family unit so we could find a sense of normalcy. A fight when the pain or medication caused her to make irrational decisions or do things that we knew were not in her best interest.

There was a lot of fighting. Not in the sense of her against us but in the sense of us against the mystery. It changed her. It changed us. While it drove us together in the fight, we lost each other along the way. We lost the connection to each other that was based on love and mutual respect. We lost so much in our fight. It was not until today that I realized... I had to lose my daughter to get her back.

It has been just over a month now that she has been gone. In that month, the emotions, the tears, everything has been all over the map. It has been hard to focus, to make any semblance of sense of it all. Why am I able to rise each day at all? Why can I move forward with any positivity? Why...?

The only answer that makes any sense is, I have my daughter back. My Madi, my Bubbles, has returned to her rightful place in my heart, if not my presence. She is once again the exuberant, positive, laughing, smiling tough kid that will walk with me the rest of my days and guide me in this uncertain journey through pain of an entirely different sort. The pain that comes from grief, from anger, from a lack of answers and the search for reason.

I had to lose my daughter to get her back. I love her more today than ever before.

CHAPTER 16

"The Rest of the Story"

The rest of the story was meant to be my annual present to Madi every Valentine's Day. While she lived it, she never got to read about it...

Later that year, on her twenty first birthday, what she did get to read was a special one of a kind gift that only I could give......

The Joy of My Heart
To Madi

Twenty-one years ago, the joy of my heart arrived in the most beautiful tiny package and I was never the same.

Every breath, every thought, every action was focused on protecting that joy, cultivating, and shaping it for the day it would stand on its own.

Today I give you that joy and my heart to carry with you for the rest of your days.

It is no longer mine to protect to cultivate or shape.

My deepest hopes and prayers are that you will carry the joy of my heart with honor pride and the knowledge that what has freely been given can never be rescinded.

It will, however, be nourished and replenished by the way you carry it, treasure it and respect it.

With ALL my love,

Daddy

The Joy of my Heart would be the last birthday present I would ever give her. The 21 years we had together was magical.

Madi Ferris, from *(In) Sane in Chronic Pain* blog:

"A letter from sick kid to sick kid"

February 25, 2017

"I want you to know you never have to apologize to anyone because of your illness. You do not owe the world an explanation. You are stronger than most of the human race and you will get thought this. You will manage it; you will handle it you will conquer it. And after everything that I have said, THE most important thing is that you know you are a badass human being."

Madi's Memorial Garden with fountain, built by Dad and EJ to honor Bubbles.

Memories of Madi

When you lose someone, your collective future is erased. What cannot be erased, however, are the memories. Not just the memories that you shared with them, but the memories they created with others. Knowing how Madi impacted those around her and the joy that she shared with everyone has allowed my heart to move forward by taking pride in the past.

"I held Madeline the day she was born. That girl could turn the world on with her smile. She was a goof with an infectious giggle and a huge heart. I loved being her "Aunt".
~~Sally, mom's best friend.

"When I think of Madi, I think of her laugh. She would giggle with her friends and was always at the house with Kaitie. She loved horses. She, Kaitie, and Lauren had so many good times playing in the neighborhood with EJ tagging along. Madi was a happy, beautiful girl with an infectious smile. We love and miss your beautiful girl.
~~Jill, 2nd grade teacher and friend's mom.

"I remember Madi's smile. It was the first thing I noticed about her and thought how happy she was. Madi was always polite and had impeccable manners. Maybe because I was so much older, LOL, but to meet someone so young that treated me with such kindness and acceptance made me feel at ease with her. We became friends. We would spend time together every couple of months. We would talk about everything under

the sun. She was always someone that I loved seeing, such a beautiful soul. Looking back and learning about her health issues and now knowing how much pain she was in makes me admire her to no end. Never, ever did she complain or let me know that she was ever in pain or had any health problems. She told me of her future plans and going through with her live even though she had setbacks. Even then it was not complaining, it was very matter of fact. Madi let me adopt her beautiful Cocker Spaniel, Ava. Ava was an amazing beautiful dog just like Madi was an amazing beautiful girl. I miss them both and picture them playing together today."
~~John, friend and hairstylist

"I had the amazing pleasure of meeting Madeline Ferris the Fall before her senior year. She was a joy filled amazing young woman who filled the room with smiles and laughter. Because of her health issues, she was looking for a school to finish her senior year that could give her time to rest and still be on campus. Madi was a bit apprehensive when I told her the only science class was Anatomy and Physiology. After the first class, she was hooked! Her passion for learning and for life was unreal. It was inspirational. Despite the fact she was constantly dealing with pain, she was full of joy and love! She was pure joy! Later that year our new school was going through our first accreditation visit. We discovered that because Madi was with us, we qualified as having a senior class and received our accreditation. She was always blessing people with her life, her heart, and her love. One thing that was never in doubt with Madi was her love for her family.

~~Jamie, Head of School

"Madi's smile was contagious. No matter the pain or discomfort or events that she was taking on. Her view of life was one of a kind. Madi would always rise above, even through the crooked roads and the many obstacles she faced. She was inspirational to many and made an impact on her friends and every person she came in contact with. That is the Madi I knew. The Madi I loved. The view on life that I will always try to live by. She is always with us and will always be my guardian angel."

~~Kali, teammate, and friend

"When we were younger, Madi and I would watch "Parent Trap" in one of our RV's during softball tournaments. She was the first pitcher I ever called pitches for as a catcher and I loved when she would learn a new pitch we could practice together. She is and always will be my favorite person I ever caught for. She was full of laughter, sarcasm, and life. She is exactly the kind of person you want on your team, both in softball and in life."

~~Lindsey, teammate, and friend.

"Madi was more than just my best friend, she was like my sister. If it wasn't for her, I would never have excelled the way I did in softball or life. She pushed me to be better. She believed in me. She made me believe in myself on and off the softball

148

field. Aside from all the crazy and wild adventures we had; she taught me so much about life and cherishing our memories. She taught me to live life to the fullest. Madi was the most selfless, outgoing, and positive person I've ever known. I will forever live my life for you, Madi, and honor you every step of the way. I have you to thank for everything."
~~Brandi, friend and teammate.

"Madi, the first time I met you we were watching a hockey game...I still remember your beautiful smile, bubbly and free-spirited personality, only to find out you were living with horrible pain. We didn't get a chance to know each other long, but you made an impact on my life. I will never forget your strong-willed personality. Thank you Madi for crossing my path."
~~Sylvie, Hockey Mom

"I met Madi in the most unexpected way. We met in the migraine headache unit at St. Joseph's Hospital in Chicago. From the moment I met her, she was silly, free-spirited, and caring. Even when she was in excruciating pain, she would ask how others were doing. That was just Madi. She cared so much about other people. Madi and I were each other's outlets. We understood the pain the other was going through. No matter the time of day we could text each other to talk through the agony. We were each other's support system for our pain and the things life threw at us. She made my life brighter and I miss her friendship every single day."
~~Sammie, friend and fellow Spoonie.

"Madi and I were best friends back in the days of school-time naps and crayons. She was the neighborhood friend I could always turn to for a little mischievous (but always innocent) fun. My favorite memory with her was the day she suggested we use my remote-control spy robot to eavesdrop on my neighbor, who was a cute teenage boy across the street. We first stood in my driveway and steered it towards his house, but the robot moved too slowly and loudly. Instead, we picked it up, sprinted across the street, hid it in the flowerpot in his front yard, then sprinted back to my yard to hide. He walked out with his girlfriend. They both immediately saw the robot and us hiding and giggling across the street. Needless to say, we did not record anything juicy, but had a good laugh. This story best embodies Madi's silliness and sense of humor."
~~Lauren, childhood best friend.

"Madi was my favorite of Lauren's friends, so I always s found a way to play with them as kids. If not at our neighborhood playground, Madi would want to play tag, hide and go seek, or some other active game. She was a ball of energy that made growing up in an ordinary neighborhood memorable."
~~Ali, Lauren's little sister

"One word to describe Madi is bubbly. Her smile and laughter were contagious. There was never a dull moment with her around. We could always count on Madi to bring joy into our household."
~~Janice and Doug, Lauren's parents.

"For me, Madi's memory is combined with the relationship I witnessed since 2002. During that time period, I had 3 children and I reflect back on you both over the years, my children, and how stories we shared were relatable to my current or upcoming experiences. Simple stories mostly revolving around sports, and later on not so simple stories about the struggle. The one thing that will live with me forever is witnessing you fight for Madi. Fight is the midst of the unknown, but never giving up, never accepting no for an answer, and the unconditional love for her. As a father, I understand completely, but wish that fight on no one. The memory of Madi that stays with me forever is simply her smile. Her smile was welcoming and comfortable. The last time I saw her, breakfast at the Coffee House Café, that smile as we discussed a little bit of life and cars, is the memory of Madi that will live with me forever."
~~ Todd, friend and Ed's boss

"My fondest memory of Madi was her infectious smile. I can still imagine her smile today. Madi was the kind of kid that made your day brighter simply by being herself. From time to time, the classroom light & noise would aggravate Madi's symptoms, so she would work on her studies in the front office with me. Even though I knew she wasn't feeling well, she always persevered through her pain to keep up with her schoolwork. Madi's strength & sheer tenacity were to be marveled. There are people who come & go throughout your life, some you remember, some you don't. Madi is someone that I will never forget.

Her memory will live on in the lives of those she touched."
--Laura, High School Business Manager

"Madi's dedication & competitive spirit pushed her to compete against the strongest softball teams throughout her career. She was always willing to learn new things & strive to succeed. Madi was always smiling. She had the best & most contagious laugh & was very quick witted. I really enjoyed coaching her. Everyone comes into your life for a reason. We thank God for bringing Madi into ours, though for a short time, she left a lasting impression on our hearts. We will never forget you #16."
~~Kenny, SLAM Head Coach

"I always remember her smile & her laugh! She was great with EJ....I know with siblings that is not always 100% of the time but everyone knew she loved him deeply. And she was very quick witted! Made me laugh a lot!"
~~Holly, Wife of SLAM Head Coach
"Madi was a quiet, calm and soothing force among our group. A force that was sorely missed when she was no longer with us. She was brilliant and resilient. She had one of the sweetest souls I have ever known. Madi was one of the friendliest people I will never forget. Rest in paradise, sweet girl."
~~ Asun, high school friend

Hard to Believe....
>It's been 30 days since you've gone away
>Not a single one of them has gone by
>Where I didn't break down and cry
>It's been 30 days since you've gone away

>Our lives will never be the same
>Your smile, your laugh, your amazing flair
>The Love you gave had no compare
>Our lives will never be the same

>It's been 30 days since you've gone away
>The emptiness, pain, longing, and grief
>My heart is hurting and there is no relief.
>Our lives will never be the same.
>>Hard to Believe...

>Spirit in Our Eyes
>Spirit in the Sky
>by Jim Ferris

There is a hole in the world where joy used to be.
It was not a static spot but travelled from place to
place. From home to school to doctor's visits.
In its wake were smiles and laughter and tears
through the pain.
And hope. Hope that the living nightmare would
vanish as suddenly as it appeared.

Those who have faith understand and reassure
one another, though the body may be destroyed,
the spirit persists.

Most often this comes to mind at a time such as
this. When family and friends, old and new, gather
in memorial.

But we do not need to call it Faith. We witnessed a body ravaged, a future stolen, a promise left unfulfilled.

At each juncture, the undaunted spirit persevered, the glory of its strength shone through.
And we know this spirit lives.

We call her, Madi.

THE END

CPSIA information can be obtained
at www.ICGtesting.com
Printed in the USA
LVHW081928170920
666328LV00007B/455